*Curiosi*

# MAINE
# CURIOSITIES

## QUIRKY CHARACTERS, ROADSIDE ODDITIES
## & OTHER OFFBEAT STUFF

*TIM SAMPLE*
*AND STEVE BITHER*

The
Globe
Pequot
Press

*GUILFORD, CONNECTICUT*

**Front cover photos:** Tim Sample

**Back cover photo:** courtesy Jane Burke, photo © Rich Entel

**Cover design:** Libby Kingsbury

**Text design:** Bill Brown

**Photo credits:** p. iv, courtesy Bennett's Gems and Jewelry, photo by Kim S. Dunn; p. 8, courtesy Jane Burke, photo © Rich Entel; p. 13, courtesy Paul Vestel, photo by Jared Vestel; p. 27, photo by Win © Sommerfeld; p. 29, courtesy Bennett's Gems and Jewelry; p. 53, courtesy Farnsworth Art Museum, photo by Maureen (Leonard) Campbell; p. 56, courtesy WERU Radio Station; p. 63, courtesy Bill and Kathleen Hallinan; p. 69, courtesy L.L. Bean; p. 95 (religious statues), photo © Jere DeWaters; p. 100, photo © Michael A. Clark; p. 115, courtesy Maine Scene Inc., photo © Lyman Owen; p. 120, courtesy Graycook Productions, photo by Will Cook; p. 141, photo © Jere DeWaters; p. 148, courtesy Shakers Sabbathday Lake Community; p. 153, courtesy Red Arrow Snowmobile Club, photos by Dana Deprey; p. 175, courtesy Maine Scene Inc.; p. 176, courtesy Maine Scene Inc., photo by Lyman Owen; p. 184, courtesy Joe Perham; p. 204, photo © DeLorme; p. 207, photo © Jere DeWaters; p. 212 (top), courtesy Tim Sample, photo by Kevin Garner Wilcox, White Pine Photography; p. 212 (bottom), courtesy Steve Bither, photo by Maurice Pope. All other photos courtesy of the authors.

Lyrics on page 9 from the songs "La-De-Da" and "Fixer-Upper" from the CD *Pop Tart* by Jane Loves Maine © 2001 Jane Burke.

**Library of Congress Cataloging-in-Publication Data is available.**

ISBN 0-7627-0941-3

Manufactured in the United States of America
First Edition/Third Printing

*For my great and good friend,*
*Ms. Kevin Garner Wilcox.*
*Her warm heart, matchless wit, and boundless curiosity*
*inspired this work.*

# CONTENTS

*You were expecting maybe a lobster? Tim Sample poses with one of the more unexpected roadside attractions in Maine, "Pink Floyd" at Bennett's Gems and Jewelry in Belfast.*

# SO YOU THINK
# YOU KNOW MAINE?

**B**ack in the early 1980s (is it possible that that was twenty years ago?), I spent a couple of seasons hosting a weekly game show on Maine public television. The show, called "So You Think You Know Maine?," was essentially a Maine trivia contest. Each week, the defending champion from last week's show would return to face three new contestants in a mental slugfest to determine which of them could most rapidly provide a correct answer to such cranium strainers as "In what Maine town was the earmuff invented?" and "Who is the Moxie Man?" (You'll find the answers to both of these questions and many more within the pages of this book.) Naturally, since I had all the answers written on a batch of 3-by-5 cards, I always came off looking like the guy who knew it all.

Fast-forward to the summer of 2000. According to my editor, Laura Strom, when the folks at The Globe Pequot Press started looking around for a writer to tackle a book on Maine's "Quirky Characters, Roadside Oddities, and Other Offbeat Stuff," a lot of people pointed in my direction. Ah, the magic of television.

In many ways I suppose I was the natural choice for this assignment. (I was certainly flattered to get the offer.) Besides being born and raised here, I've spent virtually all of my adult life driving from one end of the state to the other, talking with and listening to my fellow Mainers and generally noticing and commenting on the state of the state. Although I've enjoyed traveling outside of Maine over the past half century, I've never actually lived (or, for that matter, *wanted* to live) anywhere else. In fact, perhaps the one common thread that has run through my whole career—as a Down East humorist, writer, illustrator, and correspondent for CBS News Sunday Morning—has been a running commentary on Maine, Maine people, and the Maine way of life.

*Mainers are . . .*

*. . . creative . . .*

*. . . individualistic . . .*

So I signed on the dotted line and actually started writing this book. I was soon reminded of a scene from one of Robert B. Parker's wonderful detective novels featuring the famous Boston-based gumshoe Spenser. In the book, some shadowy underworld character, upon hearing that our hero is out looking for him, describes Spenser this way: "The guy's about half as good as he thinks he is . . . but, that's still pretty good." I can certainly relate to that. It didn't take me long to discover that when it comes to Maine's Quirky Characters, Roadside Oddities, and Other Offbeat Stuff, I knew about half as much as I thought I knew . . . but that's still quite a lot.

A few months into the project (with what suddenly seemed like a ridiculously optimistic publishing deadline looming ever closer), I began realizing that perhaps I'd bitten off a bit more than I could chew. The long-suffering Ms. Strom was obviously thinking along the same lines. She began tossing a few discreet inquiries in my direction. Fortunately, by the time she got around to asking point-blank, "Do you think you could use a little help with this book?" my initial hubris had been replaced by good old-fashioned Yankee pragmatism. Yeah, I could use a hand. Once I'd finally admitted it, I knew exactly whose hand to reach for.

I've known Steve Bither for thirty years or so. Long before he gained fame as a singer/songwriter/keyboard player for that popular Maine musical-comedy institution The Wicked Good Band, Steve and I were performing together, writing songs, and creating original Maine humor comedy skits. Back in the '70s, when Steve was the piano player and I was the lead singer for The Dubious Brothers, we never failed to crack each other up onstage. This was probably a good thing since, as I recall, the sparse audiences in the joints we played back then were often otherwise occupied. Any interest they might have had in our snappy onstage patter was inevitably eclipsed by some combination of anonymous romance, anesthetic drinking, bare-knuckle pugilism, and pinball.

In the intervening years, Steve and his Wicked Good band-mates have created a bunch of popular recordings, appeared

*. . . wacky . . .*

on numerous radio and TV shows, and written *The Wicked Good Book,* a hilarious compendium of off-the-wall Maine humor that topped the statewide best-seller lists for months on end a few years back. Somewhere along the line he also managed to pick up a law degree. Smart guy. Funny, too.

So Steve and I really had a wonderful time working on this book together. We drove many miles of Maine back roads, snapped pictures, asked lots of impertinent questions, and reported back to each other each week with plenty of surprising results. In many ways, creating this book was a voyage of rediscovery into the endlessly changing landscape of our native state.

For every Perry's Nut House and Moody's Diner (venerable Maine roadside institutions we figured we already knew something about), there was a Babb's Bridge and a Gadabout Gaddis Airport waiting to be discovered around the next bend. It soon became clear that the search for Quirky Characters, Roadside Oddities, and Offbeat Stuff in the state of Maine is virtually an unending journey. I'll resist the urge to say "You can't get there from here." But, like the famous China, Paris, Norway, and Peru (Maine, that is) that Steve writes about in his story on Lynchville, getting there isn't even the point. It's what you see along the way that makes the journey memorable.

What we saw, and what you'll end up seeing, if you're willing to take some time to poke around the nooks and crannies of the Maine coast and venture inland for a day or two, is that Mainers are pretty committed to being creative, individualistic, wacky, and eccentric. For one thing, the lines between cultch and culture are so blurred around here that, once you've sampled our local version, you may never be able to get

*. . . and eccentric.*

'em straight again. After you've spent a few minutes talking to the Greenville man who makes "high fashion" jewelry out of moose droppings, you may find yourself wondering why his creations aren't on display in Tiffany's New York showroom. One visit to the Down East Museum of Natural History and you'll wonder what all the fuss is about down at the Smithsonian. You get the idea.

Although Steve and I have done our very best to introduce you to many—perhaps even most—of the more off-the-wall attractions of our great state, we don't want you to think that this book is the final word on the subject. We sincerely hope that our collection of Maine Oddities will whet your appetite for more of the same. This is just the tip of the iceberg, folks. As long as there are long, cold winters followed by tourist-jammed summers, you can bet that Mainers will continue to create newer, better, and more outlandish roadside attractions. Why do we do it? Who knows. Maybe it's just to get you to stop and ask directions to the next roadside attraction. Ayuh, that's probably it. We always get a kick out of it when you ask directions.

Tim Sample
Razor's Edge Farm
Georgetown Island, Maine

## THE TELSTAR BUBBLE
### Andover

The little town of Andover wasn't even on the map until the bubble came. "You'd see Byron and Rumford, but the town of Andover was so small they wouldn't even put it on most maps," said Roger, a guy I happened to meet, who grew up in Andover in the 1950s and 1960s. Back then the town was so small that Roger's graduating class of seventeen was the largest in Andover High School history. Everything changed when Andover became the site, in the early 1960s, of TXX1, a tracking antenna for one of the earliest communications satellites, Telstar. America was just entering the space age in those days. The Tornados' song, "Telstar," with its space age organ and guitar sounds, was the rage. And, with the making of a space bubble, Andover was put on the map.

The engineers at Bell Labs developed the antenna-satellite system, along with government-funded Project Relay, using parts from the *Nike, Zeus,* and *Hercules* rocket systems. (No, they didn't have "swooshes" on them.) The engineers needed a location free from the interference of microwave and other transmissions. Andover sat in a natural bowl, and it was thought that the microwaves wouldn't interfere with the operation of the station. A sensitive antenna, or horn, was constructed for the transmission of telephone, television, and data communications between outer space and Andover. The most interesting part of the scheme was "the bubble": Built of treated canvas, the giant bubble was designed to keep the elements of weather off the antenna.

The bubble brought opportunities for local involvement. Local workers made top dollar clearing the land for the bubble. At first, the public was invited inside the bubble to gawk at the antenna, but the constant traffic had an impact on the atmospheric pressure inside. So the "bubbleites" (as they were called) built a viewing area, a "fishbowl," to observe the antenna horn as it circled on its track following an invisible star. Some folks in town were less than excited about the bubble; they thought the project was a waste of government money. Other folks were certain the government was doing something it wasn't telling us about, and that UFOs were being tracked. Some folks, whether they were local or not, took potshots at the bubble with their hunting rifles (at least, they said, they couldn't miss hitting this). David Belanger, who worked at the bubble and now works at the communications site, said a crew once counted seven bullet holes in the skin of the bubble.

At its heyday, the station employed about ninety people, many of them professionals from New York and other foreign lands. These people built nice homes and brought some money into town. Naturally, they also brought with them their own views of how things should be run locally, which caused some resentment.

By the 1980s the bubble had outlasted its usefulness. Newer forms of satellite dishes withstood the elements better. According to David, it cost $100,000 to heat the bubble, which made it economically unfeasible. In 1985, the bubble was decommissioned. Then it was dismantled. "Al Bancroft, a local resident, tore it down and took the scrap metal to the junkyard," says David. Local people took discarded lights and doorknobs from the site, and some folks actually took chunks of the bubble as souvenirs of the early space age. So, if you're looking for the bubble, you'll find it in pieces in local barns. The cutting-edge technology that got the station going was replaced by fiber optics. Now owned by WorldCom, the antenna traffic is focused on transmitting to countries whose infrastructures are not as up-to-date as ours. The antenna station, no longer in a bubble, employs about seven people.

The high-tech antenna in the bubble has its ironic side. It must be remembered that the bubble's antenna was plunked down in the middle of relatively undeveloped countryside. Roger remembers that, in the early '60s, if you had a good, strong TV antenna, and if it wasn't cloudy on the mountaintop, you might be able to get two or three of the Portland TV stations. As for telephones, David Belanger recalls an incident when he was in the service, stationed in Texas. He wanted to call his girlfriend back home, and he had to go through a series of operators to request a connection to "6–ring–3." This was the number to call on the multiparty crank telephones that the townspeople were still using. The Andover operator told David, "Oh, I just saw her [his girlfriend] walking by; she'll be at another number. I'll ring her up there for you." Which she did, and the connection was made in a way that antennas and bubbles still may not be able to do.

## D U K E ' S   B A R B E R   P O L L :
## A S   M A I N E   G O E S ,   S O   G O E S   T H E   N A T I O N
### *A u g u s t a*

**O**f course, it's always easy to be a Monday morning quarterback on these things. Still, I feel pretty confident in saying that if Dan Rather and the rest of the network TV news anchors had taken the time to put their high-priced consultants on hold for five minutes and make a call to Augusta, Maine, on Election Night 2000, they all might have ended up with a lot less egg on their collective faces.

Like it or not, exit polls and other forms of modern-day prognostication have become an integral part of election news coverage. Taking the public pulse in this manner is a multibillion dollar business. But, as the flip-flopping predictions of newscasters in our most recent presidential elections pointed out, sometimes even the most scientific poll results that money can buy are embarrassingly off the mark.

Which brings us to Duke Dulac, who, for the better part of forty years, has been "lowering ears" at Duke's Barber Shop, which is located alongside the traffic rotary on the west side of the Kennebec River in Augusta. You want accuracy in your political polls? You got it at Duke's. For the past twenty-seven years, besides cutting hair (three chairs, no waiting), Duke has been polling his customers and using their ballots to predict the outcome of upcoming elections. How's his track record so far? Actually, it's perfect, thank you very much. That's right, when it comes to calling the winner of the race for the White House, Duke's "barber poll" has a 100 percent rate of accuracy. Not impressed? Since instituting his decidedly unscientific survey back in 1973, he's also had a 100 percent success rate in predicting the outcome of Maine's gubernatorial races. If you factor in races for the Senate and House of Representatives, local and statewide offices, and the inevitable referendum issues that are so popular here in the Pine Tree State, his poll still boasts an astounding 97 percent success rate.

A case in point: According to Duke, "When Cohen [Senator and later Secretary of Defense William Cohen of Bangor] ran against Libby Mitchell in '84, he came in and I gave him a printout of how he was gonna do. Out of 350 people, we had him getting 87 percent of the vote and Libby 13 percent. It came out he ended up getting 86 percent and Libby 14 percent. He sent me a letter a couple days after the election that said, 'Nice job, Duke. Try harder next time. You were off one point.' So I said to him when I saw him at Jock's [former Maine Governor John "Jock" McKernan] inauguration, we were off one point because you went home and took a nap after I showed you how well you were doing!"

What's he doing that all the big shots aren't? Well, according to Duke, it's just common sense. He believes that when people are contacted by telephone pollsters, they know that somehow these folks got a hold of their phone number, and, despite

*Hairstyles are fickle. But Duke Dulac's "Barber Pole" is never wrong!*

assurances of anonymity, their responses tend to be influenced by what they think the caller wants to hear. According to Duke, the same is true with exit polls. For instance, in the weeks prior to a statewide vote on a gay rights referendum in Maine ("A touchy one," says Duke), virtually all the polls showed the bill passing by a comfortable margin. Duke's customers accurately predicted its defeat. Duke figures that since people didn't want to be branded homophobes, they said whatever they thought a questioner wanted to hear. But in the privacy of the voting booth they voted the way they really thought. The results may not have been the best reflection on Mainers' social attitudes, but they sure were accurate.

How private is the barber poll? Voting at Duke's is virtually identical to the real thing. He uses real ballots obtained from the city, the same ones people will see when they step into the booth. ("Sometimes they'll stamp 'sample' on 'em," he says.) And the process is completely anonymous. Instead of perusing a three-month-old copy of *Field and Stream* or *Sports Illustrated*, customers perched on the chrome-and-vinyl chairs lining the south wall simply mark their ballots, fold them in half, and drop them in the official ballot box. No one sticks a camera in their face and asks them how they voted. Nobody knows their phone number or mailing address. No salesman will call.

Duke figures that his clientele is a pretty representative cross section of average Maine folks. Consequently, when the ballots are counted at the end of the day, Duke knows what the people of Maine are thinking. Let's just say it's awfully hard to argue with his track record. By the way, Duke didn't spend any time agonizing along with the rest of us over the unprecedented Bush/Gore presidential election cliffhanger: He knew who the winner would be at least three weeks before election night. When it comes to picking the next president, Duke has never, *ever*, been wrong.

## *JANE BURKE LOVES MAINE*
## *(AND VICE VERSA)*
### *Augusta*

**J**ane Burke describes her tiny, campy, turquoise-and-white, kitsch-laden 1957 Vagabond house trailer as "a silver bullet lodged in the throat of state government." That statement refers to the fact that Jane's trailer, a virtual shrine to her fabulous, trademark off-the-wall visual style, is tucked away on a secluded lot, just a stone's throw from the capitol in Augusta. Not that Jane is throwing any stones, ever. She's a lot more likely to pick 'em up, paint 'em Day-Glo orange, and line her driveway with 'em.

No pop star from A(retha) to Z(appa), ever had a better time playing in the fields of popular "kulchah" than Jane Burke. Jane's whole raison d'être since she arrived on this planet seems to have been inventing, reinventing, and re-reinventing herself and reinterpreting the world around her. She claims to do this mostly for her own amusement. But it also serves as great entertainment for those lucky passersby who stray into her highly charged, brilliantly hued force field.

According to Jane, her adolescence was characterized by a "need for notoriety." It's hard to argue that point with a woman who walks around with half of her hair dyed a brassy blond and the other half a generic brown. Of her hairstyle, Jane simply states, "I had to entertain myself." Early in her career, in the absence of any volunteers, Jane started her own Jane Burke Fan Club, complete with regular newsletters describing her day-to-day activities—applying makeup, raking blueberries, that sort of thing.

*Impersonating a Maine lawn ornament is but one of
Jane Burke's many talents.*

You can laugh all you want (believe me, Jane would approve),
but eventually some pretty high-profile people ended up on the
Jane Burke bandwagon. A few summers back actress Kirstie
Alley became a fan. "I painted a lot of furniture for her home
here in Maine," says Jane. "And I painted murals for the children." After thoroughly Jane Burke–izing her place in Maine,
Alley persuaded Jane to leave the state of Maine (not an easy
thing to do), and our heroine spent several months painting furniture, murals, and other stuff in the star's California home.

After finishing up out west, she headed to New York to col-
laborate with some other decorative painters on the former
apartment of the late legendary screen idol Greta Garbo. But as
outrageously attention-grabbing as Jane can be, at heart she's a
"serious" artist with zero interest in coasting along with the
"artist to the stars" bit. "I'm really uncomfortable with that

whole thing," says Jane. In L.A., she says, "so many people seemed to be, like, in awe about all celebrities. It really bothered me." It also bothered her that folks took her art more seriously just because she had worked for a "big-name star."

Whatever Jane has done with her creativity, it's the opposite of selling out. For her, creativity is a calling, almost like a religion, and she has little patience with those who view art as an after-thought. According to Jane, "If you put the beauty, the creativity, THE ART first, then the other things will eventually . . . ." She pauses. "Well," she says, "you're not gonna starve."

But you might come close. Jane talked to me matter-of-factly about the time she had to choose between buying food and pur-chasing a cassette of new music she wanted to listen to. She chose to feed her soul. Clearly, she made the right choice.

These days Jane is justifiably excited about the release of her new (over a decade in the making) CD entitled *Pop Tart* (record-ed with her band, Jane Loves Maine). Oh, yeah, did I forget to mention that Jane Burke is a fine poet and songwriter? There's just a lot goin' on with this Maine Grrrrlll, that's all. Amazingly, the CD manages to capture a good deal of the eclectic, funny, off-the-wall, infectious, life-affirming charisma of Jane Burke. I can't explain what the music sounds like, OK? But here's a smat-tering of lyrics from the song "La-De-Da" that could only have come from the bright interior of Jane Burke's brain:

> *Your dry land I'll saturate, your defenses penetrate. I'll implicate you like a bloody glove.*

She may well be the most visually oriented person you've ever met. But, with Jane Burke there's always more going on than meets the eye. On her song "Fixer-Upper" (in which Me. stands for the two-letter postal abbreviation for Maine), she sings:

> *Took a vow of laughter, dead serious about life,*
> *never been a mother, never been a wife,*
> *I'm in love, in love, in love with Me.*

Apparently "Me." thinks you're OK, too, Jane.

Border with Quebec, Canada: 292 miles

Border with New Brunswick, Canada: 319 miles

Border with New Hampshire: 140 miles (but it costs you a buck to get there)

Maine coastline (nooks and crannies): 3,460 miles

# BORDER TRIVIA

**M**aine is basically diamond-shaped, with four major sides. As we learned in school, it is the only state in the continental United States that has only one other state bordering it. (Maine is also the only state with one syllable—you could look that up.)

According to the Maine Department of Transportation and the International Boundary Commission, Maine's borders look like this:

## E*LVIS* C*OMES* T*O* M*AINE*
### *Augusta*

The brass plaque in the lobby of the Augusta Civic Center commemorates the evening of May 24, 1977. That date marks the only Maine appearance of "The King," rock 'n' roll pioneer Elvis Presley. The legendary zeal of Elvis's fans being what it is, I just assumed that the dull, worn spots on the left side of the plaque were the result of thousands of true believers lovingly caressing its polished surface. Dave Jowdry, who manages the facility, acknowledges that that's what a lot of folks think. It makes a great story, he says. But the truth is a bit more pedestrian.

The shrine was apparently defaced when some overly enthusiastic Republicans (obviously not Presley fans) hastily taped a campaign sign to its surface during a convention a few years back. Not to worry, says Dave (who attended the Elvis show and, although he never met the man, is proud to say that he glimpsed the back of The King's head backstage surrounded by a phalanx of the Memphis Mafia). The Maine Elvis fan club is raising funds for a shiny new replacement, which should be arriving soon.

Brief though his sojourn in Maine was, Elvis left some lasting impressions. After the show in Augusta, he spent the night at the Sheraton Tara in South Portland. According to longtime Sheraton employee Mavis Spaltro, Elvis and his entourage took over the entire eighth and ninth floors of the East Tower. The King himself was ensconced in Room 807. No employees were allowed on the floor with Elvis during his stay. Nevertheless, several managed to glimpse—you guessed it—the back of his head. That famous head presumably spent at least some time on the bathroom floor, since when he left, the management found Elvis's autograph on the underside of the sink. By the way, if you're a hard-core fan you can still book Room 807. But the sink is gone, torn out and auctioned off as a souvenir during renovations several years back.

Like his legendary life, the Elvis in Maine story ends on a blue note. Elvis was booked at the same hotel for his second Maine appearance on August 16, 1977, the very day he was found dead in his home at Graceland.

### *WHO YA GONNA CALL? PAUL VESTAL*
#### *Bangor*

If you tend to be a typecaster, you know, one of those people who makes snap judgments about folks based on outward appearances, you generally won't fare all that well in the state of Maine. But Bangor's Paul Vestal may very well be your worst nightmare. Sitting bare chested and tattooed astride his vintage Harley, Paul is the spitting image of the guys your mom warned you about, the "rebel without a clue" types just born to raise hell.

I tend to be pretty open-minded about these things, but even I was taken aback by this guy. When I first met Paul many years ago at a statewide gathering of five thousand-plus leather-clad, Hog-straddling bikers (the United Bikers of Maine Annual Toy Run for underprivileged kids), I figured him for a classic wrong-side-of-the-tracks hellraiser. Imagine my surprise when I learned that he had just recently retired as the warden of the state maximum-security prison in Thomaston. This man, who was as proud of the 180,000 miles he had personally logged on his customized Harley chopper as he was of his "Flamin' Injun" tattoo (if that's not PC enough for you, please take it up with Paul and leave me out of it), was the top corrections officer in the state? Ayuh, a darn good one, too.

Paul obviously enjoys busting up stereotypes. Just as obviously he has a serious lifelong commitment to helping juvenile

*Here's one of Maine's top law enforcement professionals going out for a Sunday drive.*

offenders stay out of prison. A former member of an outlaw motorcycle gang, these days Paul tries to steer troubled teenagers toward a better way of life: "I have always been an advocate for and someone who works with primarily juveniles from 'the wrong side of the tracks' in programs that are designed to help kids who get into a lot of problems with law enforcement and mental health."

These days Paul Vestal works for Catholic Charities of Maine. "I've been with Catholic Charities about five years now," he says. "I run a variety of programs that deal with kids who either have severe mental health problems or have been busted." Paul says he tries to keep these kids out of juvenile lock-ups. He also uses his own youth as a sort of cautionary tale. "What turned me around a long time ago," he says, "was the fact that I didn't want somebody coming along and repossessing my motorcycle." Hey, apparently it's working. Paul has a good track record with these kids.

Paul Vestal may never have had his chopper repossessed, but he did play a key role in getting the grounds of the St. Michael's Center in Bangor (where his office is located) "unpossessed." "When I got here," he recollects, "they told me that there were these ghosts in the facility. Even some of the people from our central office had been run out of the building by them because they were scared of what was going on" (creaking floorboards, mysterious voices, slamming doors in vacant rooms, etc.).

"We determined that there were some graves on the property. But there were no headstones. So first off, for the first time in my career, I had to go and search for graves. Second off, when we found them, we went out and put some new headstones on the graves. Now the ghosts seem to be pretty satisfied where they are, 'cause nobody's made any mention of them since."

I figure the ghosts were just smart to quit haunting while they were ahead. After all, who wants to further tempt fate by messing around with an outlaw biker turned prison warden and Catholic youth worker who tools down the highway on a customized Harley with the line "Bat Out of Hell" lettered across the back of his jacket?

## Is Paul Bunyan Really a Mainer?
### Bangor

My best friend hails from Minnesota, so it was only natural that she was a bit skeptical when I took her to visit Bangor's famous Paul Bunyan statue and tried to convince her that the legendary giant lumberjack got his start here in the Pine Tree State. I suppose you'd get the same reaction from most Minnesotans. By all accounts, Minnesota is practically

*It's the big guy, Paul Bunyan, holding the world's biggest peavey.*

littered with Paul Bunyan statues, including an 18-footer in the town of Brainard, which was erected more than twenty years before our "Paul" and features the big guy's famous sidekick, Babe the blue ox. On the other hand, if we're talkin' big guys, Paul in Bangor would have the edge. At 31 feet, our Paul stands head and shoulders above his western rival. And if our woodsman is missing his ox, at least he's got a peavey.

What's a peavey? Well, it seems that back in 1858 a blacksmith from Stillwater, Maine (remember the name of the town, OK?), was watching the local log drivers on the Stillwater River as they separated the jammed-up logs with crude pikes. Struck by inspiration, he retired to his shop and started to hammer out his new invention. A few days later he emerged with the first peavey, a sharp iron pike attached to a long wooden handle with a hook or "dog" hanging from the underside. The peavey was a brilliantly simple tool. The leverage provided by the pike, iron hook, and long wooden handle made the dangerous task of rolling logs on the swift river easier, faster, and much safer. It was an immediate hit, and more than a century later Peavey Manufacturing is still making peaveys and selling them around the globe.

So what about Stillwater? My friend grew up next door to the town of Stillwater, Minnesota, which was founded by lumbermen who had migrated west from guess where? Ayuh . . . Stillwater, Maine. I figure those folks just brought the Paul Bunyan story to Minnesota along with 'em.

### ANNUAL BIKE BLOW
#### Bar Mills

If you happen to be driving along Route 202 4 miles west of Gorham around the first of June, don't be surprised if you see a few hundred folks standing around in a circle staring at a riderless motorcycle, its engine revving at maximum rpms, its frame shaking and shuddering, its moving parts screeching, smoking, and generally disintegrating in the middle of a muddy vacant lot. What might reasonably be mistaken for the field exercises of some offbeat cult bent on perfecting psychokinesis turns out to be the annual Bike Blow at Reynolds Motorsports.

This bizarre exercise in conspicuous consumption is the brainchild of the proprietor, Calvin "Cal" Reynolds. According to Reynolds employee Scott Lyons, the Bike Blow has been a big hit, drawing folks from all over the state for the past fifteen years or so. It goes something like this:

"We get a bike [motorcycle], usually one that's been abandoned here or just been kickin' around, and we'll drain all the oil out of it and take some duct tape and tape the throttle wide open." Like a mechanized sacrificial lamb, the motorcycle is then wheeled out into the middle of a vacant field next door. The crowd gathers to scrutinize the doomed vehicle and place bets on how long it will survive in the event. It's all in good fun, of course. But there is something a bit weird and a little unsettling about the atmosphere. The crowd's building enthusiasm, the gleam in the spectators' eyes, the eager anticipation of mayhem to come—the whole scene feels a bit like you're standing in line for a matinee performance at the ancient Roman Coliseum.

No one would accuse the Bike Blow of being overly sophisticated. The whole point is to hit the ignition, stand back, and let the engine run flat out . . . without benefit of internal lubrication, until the bike completely self-destructs. The process can take anywhere from two minutes to almost an hour. Whichever onlooker correctly predicts the moment of meltdown collects the cash, hops on his or her (presumably pampered and fastidiously maintained) motorcycle, and rides home.

Although the actual experience is kind of anticlimactic (like watching paint dry, only a lot louder), the event does have an unmistakable raw primal quality to it.

It's as if those humanoid apes in the first scene of the film *2001: A Space Odyssey* had been called in, like some hairy low-tech SWAT team, to smack the living daylights out of the smug, condescending, evil computer Hal, who shows up later in the film. Perhaps the real point is, that as long as we have events like the Bike Blow, we can all sleep a little better at night, secure in the knowledge that those nasty machines won't be taking over the world anytime soon.

# UNCLE HENRY'S SWAP 'N' SELL: A LITERARY BARGAIN

**H**ave you priced a paperback novel lately? Let's just say they've come a long way from the days of the "dime novel." If the thought of parting with nearly a ten spot for the privilege of toting the latest best-seller to the beach makes you blanch, help is on the way.

Every Thursday, for a mere buck and a half, at just about any store in Maine with a cash register, you can pick up the latest copy of Uncle Henry's Weekly Swap or Sell It Guide. What you'll get at this bargain basement price is nearly 400 pages of tiny print at a fraction of what you'd pay for the same thing from John Grisham or Stephen King.

It's not the same you say? Those folks are great storytellers? Well, I maintain there's plenty of great writing and storytelling in Uncle Henry's . . . you just have to use your imagination a bit. You see, those famous best-selling authors get paid millions for their stuff, so they can afford to sit around on their yachts, sipping champagne and spinning long complicated tales full of romance and drama, crime and punishment. But the writers you'll be reading each week in Uncle Henry's are just workin' stiffs like you and me. They can't sit around waiting for the muse to stroll in the door—they only get a half hour for lunch! Besides, the free ad form only allows you thirty words (including the town and the phone number) so Uncle Henry's writers have a built-in incentive for avoiding verbosity and complex plot lines; they just cut right to the chase. Here's just one example (and there are plenty more in each action-packed issue):

"Will swap, slightly used, size 18 wedding dress, would like to trade for 357 Magnum!" That's only fifteen words, but I think you'll agree there's a whole novel in there between the lines.

## B ELT  S ANDER  R ACES
### *Bath*

'm sure that plenty of grand schemes have been hatched over a couple of cold brews at the now defunct/always funky Triple R Bar in Bath, but it's unlikely that many of them ever developed beyond the stage of pool table banter at the legendary biker bar. The exception that proves the rule is the Belt Sander Races, which have been held regularly for the past two decades or so on the first Sunday in March at the Bath Elks Lodge. The event is run by the United Bikers of Maine, and all proceeds are donated to the Maine Children's Cancer Program.

If you're not familiar with belt sander racing, don't feel too bad. According to Mac McCreary of Woolwich, the sport is still in its infancy. Last year's turnout, one of the largest to date, included something like twenty participants and perhaps three or four times that many spectators.

McCreary's obviously a big fan of belt sander racing. (I got his phone number from an ad for the 2000 race hand painted on a sheet of plywood tacked to a toolshed in Woolwich.) He says that the inspiration for the event came in the early to mid-1980s. A bunch of local carpenters had stopped by the Triple R for a few beers on the way home from work. Some alchemy involving professional pride, alcohol, and testosterone took place, and a new sport was born. Makes sense to me. I believe that, over the years, these same conditions have contributed to the creation of many innovative recreational pursuits, everything from mud wrestling to cockroach racing.

Belt sander racers compete in either stock or modified classes on two parallel plywood tracks about 40 feet long. Rails on the sides keep these hopped-up hand tools from veering off course, and there's a thick foam rubber pad to cushion the impact at the end of the race. A lot of the contestants just use their tools

*Mainers clearly invest more in their belt sanders than in their advertising budget.*

from work. But in the modified class it's a different story. Hot rod secrets of winning belt sander racers include adding weights to the front end for traction and removing the trigger and hard-wiring the electrics for a faster start. Of course, a flashy paint job with a couple of sponsors' logos certainly doesn't hurt.

McCreary says the racers don't really have a sophisticated timing system or anything. Whichever sander smashes into the foam pad first wins. But, he estimates that a fast tool in the stock class would run the track in one and a half to two seconds, whereas a heavily modified unit might easily shave a half second off that time.

As I talked to McCreary, the date of the annual event kept bouncing around in my skull: The first Sunday in March. The first Sunday in March. Then it dawned on me. The reason why this exciting new sport would just naturally *have* to have been created here in Maine is it's a reeeealllly long winter and there just ain't a lot goin' on.

## *L o o n y  L a g o o n*
### *B a t h*

**A**ccording to Philip Day, the septuagenarian sculptor, painter, and creator of the Loony Lagoon in Bath, the inspiration for his roadside work-in-progress was a simple one: "It gives me something to do. Keeps me busy." And he certainly seems busy. Most days you can see him hauling gravel, raking leaves, generally sprucing up, and adding new creations to the zany theme-park-without-a-theme located behind his trailer. He's happy to show you around. But, like all true artists, he's more at ease creating the work than discussing it.

Other than the fact that it "keeps him busy," Day tends to be a bit tight-lipped on the subject of his creativity. When asked how he decides what characters to add to his menagerie, his response was a Zenlike "I just find somethin' that looks like somethin', and then I just make somethin'."

The range of "somethin's" to be found in the Loony Lagoon is eclectic, to say the least. There are homemade replicas of a stage coach and a bowling alley (or at least a building with a big sign to that effect tacked onto the front of it). There are also numerous witches, goblins, and ghosts hanging from the trees and standing on the shore of the lagoon itself.

Well, it's not exactly a lagoon. More like a shallow backyard mudhole, if the truth be told. Hey, the Loony Lagoon ain't Disneyland, bub! But there is something undeniably, refreshingly ridiculous about the place. The whole endeavor is really nothing more or less than one man's celebration of pure fun and unbounded imagination.

*The Loony Lagoon gives it's creator
"somethin' t' do" and the rest of us something
to look at.*

Breaching wildly in the lagoon itself is a black-and-white shark with gaping jaws squaring off against a rather happy-looking muddy brown alligator. Like all Day's creations, including oddly primitive versions of several popular big-name cartoon characters, these denizens of the shallows are rendered in glossy enamel paint on sheet aluminum.

Philip Day, a man of few words and plenty of wacky ideas, obviously disdains plywood. "Plywood don't last!" he says, passionately. "Sheets of metal and logs, that's what I use!" As if building his creatures out of anything less durable would be like carving Mount Rushmore out of plaster. Hey, who am I to argue? I figure that, when a man finally finds "somethin' to do," he darn well wants to do it right.

## A MONSTER OR A MOUSE?
### *Bath*

Charlie Cahill, Jr., opened his garage on the site of what is now Cahill's Tire Store in Bath, at the junction of Route 1 and the Old Bath Road, back in 1938. Charlie was quite a character in the community, and his son Skip has done a good job keeping up the family tradition. He's a hardworking guy who uses his lively sense of humor very effectively to lubricate the dull spots in the daily grind.

A couple of years back, Skip came up with an idea for a roadside attraction, something "a little different," that would draw passing motorists to his establishment. When you run a garage in the same location for as many years as the Cahills have, you're bound to collect a certain amount of "car junque," a used muffler here, a few spare wheels there, maybe a bit of scrap metal and a box of mismatched headlights and taillights. Hey, after a few years, it adds up. Whether the motivation was practicality (why pay somebody to lug it off?) or whimsy (more

*Skip told me he was looking for "something different."*
*I'd say he found it!*

likely, in my opinion), I can't say. But Skip decided that the growing pile of automotive castoffs would make excellent raw material for a roadside "art installation."

He enlisted the talents of local artisan John Donovan and pretty much let him go where he would with the project. The result, a four-legged, long-necked, red-eyed beast about 25 feet tall, which looks like a cross between a brontosaurus and Rudolph the Red-Nosed Reindeer, is known locally as "Skip's Monster."

You can't miss the Monster partly because of the rather sinister-looking red-tinted headlight eyeballs glowing ominously from deep within the stamped steel wheel eye sockets perched on its rust-encrusted skull. "The kids like it," says Skip, as if that were some sort of explanation. When I asked him what the public reaction to his junkyard Frankenstein has been, he told me that a lot of customers get a kick out of it. But the most interesting reaction was that of one woman from Massachusetts. According to Skip, most folks think that the Monster is actually a moose or a deer. "This lady," he said, grinning, "well now, she had a different idea." According to Cahill, she came barreling off the highway as if her car were on fire, screeched to a stop, jumped out, and with a cry of rapture exclaimed, "I love it! That's the biggest mouse I've ever seen!"

## PERRY'S TROPICAL NUT HOUSE
### *Belfast*

**S**adly, one of Maine's oldest and most venerated roadside attractions almost disappeared a few years back. Since opening its doors back in 1927, Perry's Tropical Nut House on coastal Route 1 has entertained, amused, or at least temporarily distracted tens of thousands of tourists on their annual migration.

I, for one, remember begging my mom to pull over at Perry's. As a matter of fact, the original Perry's Tropical Nut House, with its giant, gaudily painted menagerie of outsize animals standing around the parking area, was a near-perfect example of the "Hey, Mom! Can we stop in there and look around, pleeeeeeeze?" school of advertising.

Frankly, I don't recall being all that impressed with the actual store, you understand. What I do remember is that there was a certain, third-rate P. T. Barnum ambience to the whole place. There was a fair-size herd of assorted stuffed animals, most of which, if memory serves, had apparently been worked over pretty well by a roving gang of voracious moths. There were also a lot of nuts from exotic places. I don't remember that there was much in the way of formal exhibits at Perry's, just a whole lot of dusty nuts lying around in bins and cases.

Oh yeah, Perry's Tropical Nut House was also the home of the "Giant Man-Killer Clam," a huge white clamshell with a sign indicating its murderous proclivities in life. It's pretty easy for a young boy to imagine being attacked and ripped to shreds by a snarling tiger or an angry grizzly bear, but a man-killer clam? Well, maybe. Keep in mind that I first visited Perry's, as an impressionable lad, back in the fabulous '50s, an era when ants and scorpions were laying waste to entire cities down at the drive-in every weekend. In that context, I suppose a killer clam didn't seem all that far-fetched to me at the time.

I'm happy to report that Perry's opened under new management in 1997, and owner David Sleeper seems determined to restore it to its former glory. Unfortunately, most of the original exterior attractions were sent fleeing by the auctioneer's gavel (although some might yet return to their native habitat; a clerk named Bonnie told me that one of the elephants is, even now, sitting atop the Colonial Theatre in Bucksport). But Sleeper, a fan of the original Perry's, seems determined to do the right thing and has already begun rebuilding Perry's collec-

*Here at Perry's Tropical Nut House, more nuts seem
to be arriving every summer!*

tion. There's a 6-foot plush stuffed bear outside, as well as a plywood backdrop you can stick your head through while your
friends snap pictures of you giggling under the message I GOT
'CRACKED' AT PERRY'S NUT HOUSE!

I, for one, am glad to see Perry's back in business. It's hard
to tell just what the attraction of the original Perry's Tropical
Nut House was. But if I had to guess, I'd say that the name has
a lot to do with it. I think it was H. L. Mencken who once
quipped, "No one ever went broke underestimating the intelli-
gence of the American people." The ability to tell the folks back
home that, while on vacation in Maine, you stopped to visit a
"nut house" has got to be right up there with flatulence jokes in
terms of timeless appeal.

*PINK DINOSAURS ARE FRIENDLY*
*Belfast*

Creating a truly memorable roadside attraction involves coming up with something odd, goofy, or outrageous enough to smack the eyeballs of the road-weary traveler with enough force to induce the driver to pull over and visit. With any luck, you'll come up with something nobody else has thought of.

As you'll discover elsewhere in this book, there's no shortage of outsize lobsters, fishermen, etc., populating the highways and byways of Maine. So, back in the late 1980s, when Kim Dunn and Dan Bennett decided to open their gem and mineral store in Belfast, they searched for a distinctive mascot that would stand out in the crowd of slicker-clad seamen and oversize arachnids. And, by golly, they found one.

How about a pink dinosaur? Now we're talking! It seems an unlikely totem for the Maine coast, but there is some logic behind the decision. Kim explains that the dinosaur (technically, it's the skeleton of a styracosaurus, which, according to Kim, looks more friendly, feminine, and welcoming than its better-known cousin, the Triceratops) is a symbol of antiquity and geology. (Remember those fossils you studied in high school science class?) They figured that since age and geology are what gems and minerals are all about, "Floyd" would make a fine mascot for their shop, Bennett's Gems and Jewelry.

Floyd? Oh yeah, a couple of years after it was erected, Kim and Dan held a contest to name the dinosaur. The winning name was submitted by an eight-year-old girl from Minnesota who clearly had a much better knowledge of classic British '60s–'70s arena rock than her tender years would suggest.

*It's hard to believe that after all these years "Pink Floyd"*
*is still on the road.*

The original shocking pink 13-foot-long sculpture (eventually, if you sell enough Mary Kay, perhaps you could win one of these for your lawn) was painstakingly handcrafted out of pressure-treated plywood by jeweler and gem cutter Dan Bennett. It was an immediate hit. Kim says, "It pulls people right in. They can't help themselves." She also informs me that pink has been proven to be the "friendliest color," explaining that the holding cell in nearby Waldo County Jail is painted a similar color to soothe the criminal psyche while pondering one's fate.

Apparently the color wasn't quite "friendly" enough to win over a young local who wantonly decapitated the poor guy a few years back. The miscreant was eventually caught. To avoid prosecution, he agreed to assist in reattaching the ancient lizard's lopped-off cranium. Presumably, having spent some time in the company of "Pink Floyd," he ended up feeling mighty friendly about the whole thing.

## GADABOUT GADDIS AIRPORT
### Bingham

H e was a pioneer of television, a combination of Sky King, Marlon Perkins, and, maybe, the Fugitive, because he never stayed in the same place very long. He was the nicest man you'd want to know. He was Vern Gadabout Gaddis, the Flying Fisherman.

He started out as a salesman for the Shakespeare Fishing Tackle Company, then gradually got into making films and doing a radio program about fishing (remember, there also used to be a ventriloquist on the radio). As his radio show was starting, in the late 1930s, the boys who produced the show decided that his given name, Vern, just wasn't catchy enough. "Why don't you call him 'Gadabout Gaddis'?" one of the crew said. "That's a good name for him, because every time we're looking for him, he's gaddin' about the country somewhere." In 1939, an executive from NBC asked him if he wanted to try something called television. He used his fifteen minutes to show fishing movies he had made; occasionally he demonstrated fly-casting techniques. During World War II, he traveled around the world, giving demonstrations to the troops and organizing fishing expeditions. In 1963, he got his big break, when Liberty Mutual signed him to a nationwide TV series.

In the television series, you would see Gadabout Gaddis taking off in his Jeep; astute watchers would know that he was embarking from the Gadabout Gaddis Airport in Bingham, Maine.

According to Wes Baker, who organizes a fly-in to honor the memory of Gaddis, the airport was built in the 1950s and acquired by Gaddis later on. Gaddis built a home on the river, where he lived for years. He died in the mid-1980s and is buried in nearby Moscow.

Gadabout said in his autobiography, "You can believe me or not, but over the last fifty-five years, I can't remember ever having spent thirty consecutive nights under one roof. I've had the hankering to roam since I could walk, to fish since I was seven." Even though he was a gadabout, he loved the town of Bingham. Baker says, "He bought things for the town and gave money to the band. Folks in town loved him."

Gadabout Gaddis is roaming on this earth no more. But the airport is still open, now owned by a whitewater rafting firm. There is a runway of "2,000 feet, usable," according to Baker, but beyond that you wouldn't want to go. It doesn't get a lot of use, but there's a restaurant right at the airport, where folks fly in for breakfast.

Every year, the last week in September, there is a fly-in at the Gadabout Gaddis Airport. Baker says the first one, back in the late 1960s, was to honor the man who had done so much for the town; now it's an annual tradition. It's a beautiful time of year to see the northern Kennebec River. It's also a tribute to the Flying Fisherman, who wrote, at age seventy: "I've been lucky—tremendously lucky. Just the fact I've managed to live through seventy years and still feel as frisky as a pinto pony is proof enough of that. It's been a wonderful, wonderful life—even in the days when I didn't have any more than a nickel in my pocket. Wonderful? Mister, it's been the darndest life any three men together could ever have."

## OH, TO BE A "NATIVE"

**T**he moment you set foot in Maine for the first time, you will, like millions who came before you, undergo a subtle but significant transformation. Whereas formerly you had been simply a citizen of whatever state, province, county, town, or city you call home, upon entering Maine you will gain membership in that vast (something like 99.9 percent of the population of the planet) category of "people from away."

The opposite of being "from away," of course, is being a native. Native status has traditionally been a highly prized commodity in Maine, as illustrated by the old story of the two Maine farmers who had been neighbors on the same dirt road for over eighty years. Well into their nineties now, everybody just assumed they were natives. Sitting on a porch one summer afternoon, the first farmer raises the issue.

"I know everybody thinks you're a native. But I heard a rumor that you're really 'from away,'" the first farmer says.

"I hate to admit it," says the second man, "but them rumors are true. I was originally born over to New Hampshire, and I was three months old before I ever set foot in the state of Maine."

## BRUD THE HOT DOG KING:
## THESE DOGS DON'T BARK OR BITE
### *Boothbay Harbor*

**B**rud "The Hot Dog King" Pierce has been peddling wieners from his brightly painted cart on the streets of Boothbay Harbor for nearly six decades. A WW II veteran, Brud started hawking tube steak from a pushcart back in 1943. With his trademark white apron and bright orange motorized wienie wagon, Brud is almost as much a part of the architecture as the town library across from which he plies his trade. His constant commentary on the passing parade is a soliloquy worthy of a lifetime achievement award from the local chamber of commerce. "Have you been to the Railway Museum? The kids will love it! How about a boat ride? There's one leaving in about a half an hour."

*Tired of lobster? You came to the right place.*

*'Bout the only thing that's changed on this street corner*
*in the past few decades is the price of the hot dogs.*

With his eightieth birthday well behind him, Brud has
admittedly slowed up a bit. These days, between customers, he
can be found sitting in the shade on the sidewalk in his folding
director's chair with "The King" lettered across the back.
Although his step has slowed, he's still eager to recount some
of the highlights of his career, like the time back in the '50s
when dogs were selling for 20 cents a pop and he boosted his
bottom line by offering a "family special": five for a dollar!

And his wit is still as sharp and playful as ever. Mentioning
the "footbridge," a venerable local landmark connecting the east
and west sides of the harbor, he says casually to a summer visitor, "You know they aren't going to have the footbridge any
longer." Folks are inevitably dismayed. "Really?" they ask.
"Nope," says The Hot Dog King with a conspiratorial wink,
"they figure it's long enough already!"

## THIS IS DOUGIE CARTER COUNTRY
### Boothbay Harbor

Douglas "Dougie" Carter of Boothbay Harbor is pretty much everybody's idea of a Maine lobsterman straight out of central casting. He's a big rugged guy with a handsome, weather-beaten, Clint Eastwood-after-a-hard-day-in-the-saddle look about him. Behind his sandpaper-rough, Down East drawl lies a wicked yet deceptively subtle sense of humor.

Most days in the summer you can find Dougie hard at work on the waterfront. He owns his own company, The Sea Pier, a harborside lobster wharf/restaurant and wholesale/retail lobster business located on the east side of Boothbay Harbor just across the street from the Catholic church. I always try to stop in

*The Sea Pier is the place where you can find out everything you ever wanted to know about lobster but were afraid to ask.*

and pick up a fresh story when I'm in town. Here's just one
from his vast supply.

One summer afternoon, Dougie was hard at work stacking
a pile of brand-new wooden lathe–style lobster traps (the type
tourists love to lug home and turn into glass-topped coffee
tables and lawn ornaments) on the wharf. He was approached
by a rather citified tourist who obviously thought Mr. Carter
had nothing better to do than to while away the afternoon chatting with him.

"Do you s'pose I could buy one of those?" the man asked.

"I imagine," said Dougie.

"How much would you charge?"

"Oh," said Dougie, "I could let you have one of these for $75."

The tourist must have thought the price was too steep.
Without so much as a thank you, he stuck his nose in the air
and turned and walked down the pier, leaving Dougie to his
labors. A few minutes later the man was back.

"I found a pile of old traps down on the dock over there,"
the tourist said. "I was wondering whether you could give me a
better price on one of them."

"That's interestin'," said Dougie with a grin. "Matter of fact,
I'd be happy to sell you one of those old traps. But I'll have to
charge you $150 apiece for 'em." That got the tourist's attention.

"I don't get it!" the man said (never suspecting how true
that statement actually was). "Why would you charge me twice
as much for an old broken down trap as you would for one of
those brand-new ones?"

"That's easy," said Dougie. "These new traps here belong to
me. I don't know who the hell owns them old ones!"

Douglas Carter is always good for a funny tale. But when it
comes to the hard work of making a living from the sea, he
takes a backseat to no man. Dougie holds the record for the
trap-hauling competition at the Boothbay Harbor Fishermen's
Festival. He's won this event so many times (nine) that occasionally he sits on the sidelines to give somebody else a chance.
How fast is fast when it comes to lobster trap hauling? OK,

here's what it involves. Participants start out standing on the dock. At the starting gun, the lobsterman and sternman race down the dock, untie the boat, start the engine, and head out into the middle of the harbor. After rounding a marker buoy, they haul, rebait, and set six traps about 10 fathoms (60 feet) apart, race back to the dock, shut down the engine, tie up the boat, and run back up the dock to the starting line. Sounds like about a half hour of work, huh? Dougie's record is two minutes and thirteen seconds.

So if you want to meet up with an authentic Maine lobsterman, you need look no further than The Sea Pier in Boothbay Harbor. And if you decide you might want to impress your girlfriend by dickering over lobster prices with Dougie . . . well, you just go ahead and do that, sport. But, hey, don't say I never warned you.

### GIANT FIBERGLASS FISHERMAN
#### *Boothbay Harbor*

I n his authentic yellow fisherman's oilskins and sou'wester hat, the giant fiberglass fisherman standing out by the parking lot entrance at Brown's Wharf in Boothbay Harbor certainly has the look of a native Mainer. But, according to Ken Brown, who owns the place, he's actually "from away."

"We got him back in 1968, from the Amish folks down in Pennsylvania," he says. Before the statue arrived (and before Maine outlawed this kind of outdoor advertising), there was a huge billboard with a painting of a fisherman pointing his thumb in the direction of the wharf. "That one was painted by 'Linc' Rockwell," says Ken. "You know, the fascist?" He's referring to local sign painter George Lincoln Rockwell III, who gained notoriety as the head of the American Nazi Party back in the '60s and met a bad end. "Linc went out of favor," Ken

*What's big and yellow and startles tourists?*

says dryly. "Then he went out altogether. One of his henchmen shot him." Ken adds matter-of-factly, "He did do a hell of a job on the sign, though."

Ken has had plenty of fun with the statue over the years. For a while, he told me, he had the fisherman "wired up." He had installed a microphone and a speaker system running from the base of the statue to his office, enabling the fisherman to "chat" with his admirers. The "saltiest" conversations always occurred when Ken lent the office mike to some of the real fishermen who had been in the bar whetting their whistles. This practice ended some years back.

But, according to Ken, the most unique aspect of his giant fisherman statue is only visible from a certain angle. "You gotta view him from his starboard side," he says. "It's his most attractive pose. He's very proud of it. That's why he has that big smile on his face." I'll let you figure out what's so special about this view. But I'll give you a hint: It's most likely to be fully appreciated by twelve-year-old boys and fans of Mel Brooks movies.

## IS THAT A BENTLEY BEHIND DOOR NUMBER 3?
### *Brunswick*

Tibby Motors, on Old Bath Road in Brunswick, is one of those blink-and-you'll-miss-it kind of places, a modest garage/used car sales business virtually indistinguishable from a thousand others lining the roadways around small-town America. The "front line" of reasonably priced late-model sedans—Chevys, Fords, and Pontiacs—at Tibby's gives the casual observer nary a hint of what really goes on behind the row of garage doors. For the rest of the story, you've got to stop in and visit—which according to John Lee, owner and operator of Tibby's, people "who know about us" have been doing for over thirty years.

*When this man tells you "My other car is a Rolls Royce,"*
*he's not joking!*

What do those folks know that you don't? For one thing, they know that there's likely to be a beautifully restored Rolls-Royce, Bentley, or '49 TC MG roadster nestled in one of the garage bays, the sort of car most people would never see outside of an antique auto museum. These classics, many of them worth ten or twenty times as much as the most expensive vehicle for sale on the lot out front, are the passion that drives John Lee.

According to John, he got bitten by the "car bug" at an early age, back in 1959, and he's never been the same since. "The first one," he says, "was a 1916 Model T Ford. My brother and I bought a pair of them for two dollars. We've gone onward and upward from there." He added with a grin, "Pretty soon we'll get our two dollars back."

He's not kidding about the two bucks either. If you saw John and his wife, Sandy, tooling around the coast on a summer's evening in his immaculate 1926 3-liter Bentley or taking turns behind the wheel of Sandy's fabulous '38 Bentley Vanden Plas Drophead (in British classic car lingo, that means it's got a convertible top), looking for all the world like they're on their way to a cocktail party at Jay Gatsby's house, it would be easy to mistake this modest couple for the "idle rich."

In truth, they are neither. John and Sandy Lee are just obsessed with great old cars and happy to be that way. But, frankly, the way they're going, they're never going to get rich. When I asked John whether Sandy still had her lovely little green '49 MG roadster, he sighed and said, "That was a beautiful car. That went away to finance the restoration work on her Bentley." See what I mean? I asked John whether there was a Holy Grail at the end of this lifelong search. Is there any one classic car that, once purchased, he would keep and drive for the rest of his life?

"No, I don't think so," he replied. "The fellow we bought most of these Bentleys from is a man named Bill Lasseter. He lives in Florida and has a collection of about a hundred classic cars. Bill and I were standing right in the middle of them one day and I said, 'Bill, I'd like to have every car you have here.' He stepped back and looked a little surprised. Then I said, 'One at a time.' " I agree with John. He's never gonna get rich doing this. But he and Sandy have found something that makes them happy, owning, tinkering on, talking about, restoring, buying, selling, and best of all *driving* some of the world's great automobiles, one car at a time.

*So many cars, so little time.*

## *FAT BOY DRIVE-IN: HOME OF THE "WHOPER"*
### *Brunswick*

**B**efore McDonald's vast worldwide "Zillions and Zillions Served" burger empire was much more than a glint in Ray Kroc's eye, there was the Fat Boy Drive-In. In fact, when John Bolinger flipped his first burger there in 1955, the massive tailfins that would forever define the fabulous '50s had barely begun to sprout from postwar fenders.

Strange as it seems in twenty-first-century drive-thru America, the notion of eating a burger and fries in your car was a real novelty in the days of Brylcreme and doo-wop. In most cases, the novelty wore off almost as quickly as it had arrived. So how come the Fat Boy is still jammin' 'em in on a hot summer night?

Ken Burton, nephew of the original owner, has been running the place since 1983. He figures that the secret of his success is simple: good food, fast service, and Car Culture nostalgia. You'll find all of that at the Fat Boy for sure, but I think there's more to it than that. Maybe the real secret of the Fat Boy's seemingly endless summers is the quirky appeal of the Whoper Burger. You read that right. It's Whoper (pronounced WHOA-purr), not Whopper.

Fat Boy patty flippers had been cranking out something called a "whopper burger" for years when fast-food giant Burger King wrote to inform them that the name was spoken for. Rather than argue with the 800-pound gorilla, the folks at the Fat Boy, in true Maine fashion, simply lopped one *p* off their all-beef patty (the sign inside reads I KNEW THE STEER PERSONALLY) and kept on flipping. It's not like the discovery of penicillin or anything, but that moment of inspiration may just have been the key to the Fat Boy's booming success. After all, you can get good food at a lot of places, but the Fat Boy Drive-in on Old Bath Road between Bowdoin College and Cooks Corner is the only place in the entire world where you can pull into the parking lot, flash your lights for service, roll down your window, and tell the car hop (with a straight face) "I'll have the Whoper Burger, please."

## CAPTURING SHARED HISTORY ON FILM
### *Bucksport*

When Karen Sheldon and David Weiss, founders of Northeast Historic Films in Bucksport, came to Maine from Boston back in the mid-1980s, they literally had no idea what they were getting into. "Karen and I came to Maine for an experimental year, back in 1984," says David, "to see if we could figure out something we could do that would keep us from having to go back to Boston and get 'real' jobs."

Karen and David were not the first young urbanites to try this approach, and they certainly won't be the last. But despite some pretty hefty credentials in audiovisual production back in Bean Town, they found the going in Maine rather tough. "It turned out that it was pretty hard, it probably still is pretty hard, to put together a working production company up here unless you have national stature and can pull stuff in," says David.

Their big break came when Henry Nevison at the University of Maine in Orono stumbled upon a 1930s film of the last long logging operation on the Machias River. Nevison ("A one-man band up there," according to David) had the talent, but not the time, to restore the film properly. Karen and David had both, and the film restoration, the statewide screenings of the film, and a best-selling video that came later set the foundation for Northeast Historic Films.

The film, entitled *From Stump to Ship,* was shown statewide. The producers expected at best maybe a few hundred folks to

*The Maine
slogan might be
"Remember at
The Alamo."*

show up to see this cinematic curiosity of the past. Were they
ever wrong! Over 1,100 people came to the first showing. "It
was huge!" says David. "We had 800 people in Machias and 600
in Farmington. We showed it from Cape Porpoise to
Madawaska, and thousands and thousands of people turned
out." David and Karen had finally found their niche in Maine.

The genesis of their follow-up hit, *Woodsmen and River
Drivers,* is, if anything, even odder and more unlikely. "Of
those thousands of people who came to see the film," says
David, "some of them said, 'I've got a box of film at home that's
at least as good as that.' Some of them said, 'That's *me* in the

movie!' " That's right, some of the theatergoers watching *From Stump to Ship* turned out to be the very men, now in their eighties, who could be seen, flushed with youth and strength, "horsing" logs down the rapids of the Machias River right up there on the silver screen. These days, in addition to these first two films, the Northeast Historic Films catalog lists nearly a hundred products.

Now housed in the Alamo Theatre, Maine's second-oldest purpose-built movie theater (erected in 1916), Northeast Historic Films is embarking upon another quest, the collection, cataloging, and archiving of home movies. That's right, Karen and David are asking Mainers to scour attics and basements in search of forgotten reels.

Home movies of Janey and Bobby in the Fourth of July parade back in '49 are really a big deal, according to David. Although Mom and Dad never set out to be great filmmakers, David says that their moving images contain much that is of historical significance for this and future generations. "If you take the Fourth of July parade, and it goes down a street that used to be lined with elms and they've all died, well, maybe you were looking at Johnny riding his bicycle when he was six. But for anybody coming down that road today, they might well be struck by how different the town looked. We have footage of Freeport that shows L.L. Bean as this little walk-up second-floor storefront." In the end, this "accidental" documentation of important historical stuff is what Northeast Historic Films is all about. "The truth of the matter is," says David, "everybody who has taken movies has captured a bit of our shared history that will just get more and more interesting and valuable as time goes on."

I was lucky enough to meet Karen and David during the first weeks of their "experimental year" in Maine back in 1984, and I'm happy to see that they found something here that would keep them from going back to Boston and getting "real" jobs.

I can also tell you that what David says of these "accidental" films is also true of the two of them. They just get more interesting and valuable as time goes on.

## THE "BUCK" GRAVESTONE
### Bucksport

I was probably about six or seven years old when I first saw the strange markings on the large granite gravestone in Bucksport and heard the spooky tale of the Bucksport Witch. You can't miss the headstone. It's right there at the front of the cemetery on Route 1 in Bucksport. The name BUCK is carved into the granite, and you can clearly see the ghostly image of what might be (if you squint just right and use a little imagination) the image of a witch's foot like a huge watermark seeping through the smooth granite. I'll guarantee you, when you've heard the tale of the phantom foot, that stain on the granite looks pretty creepy in a "cursed from beyond the grave" sort of way. Of course, the mark might just as easily be interpreted as a ghostly image of the state of Florida (upside down and backward) or a Christmas stocking or a lot of other things. But generations of locals have stamped their imprimatur on the "witch's foot" (or leg) legend, so that's what it is.

So what is the legend of the Bucksport grave marker? Ah, that's where things start to get murky. When I tried to remember the version I'd heard as a child, I could only recall that it had something to do with a woman who had been cruelly burned at the stake for allegedly practicing witchcraft back in colonial times. That seemed pretty plausible given what I'd heard of purported puritanical excesses in that department. Also, there was something in there about the woman being falsely accused, which seemed like it was par for the course. Then there was the part about Jonathan Buck, founder of the town that bears his name and apparently the poor soul whose mortal remains are even now doing the "dust to dust" bit beneath the stone. Maybe he was responsible for the rush to

*The Buck stopped here—and so did the witch.*

justice? Maybe he was falsely accused himself? Were there, perhaps, some disgruntled "Indians" involved? Something about a
leg being snatched from the fire at the last minute?

My attempts to resolve the details only deepened the mystery. I contacted Pamela Dean at the Maine Folklife Center at
the University of Maine in Orono, and she faxed me some material. It soon became clear that the variety and diversity of the
"ghost stories" about the image on the stone resembled the list
of choices on a Chinese takeout menu, and none of them
appears to have much to do with the truth. The only thing that
seems clear from the historical record is that poor old Jonathan
Buck (a founding father and apparently a model citizen born in
1719, well after the era of colonial witch hunts) is no more than
an innocent bystander.

The rest of the characters in the various accounts include:
an innocent woman with a missing leg, the village idiot, at least
one witch, the witch's son, some local Indians, one or more ani-
mated talking corpses, vain attempts to chemically remove the
telltale leg stain, and reopened caskets with one to three legs in
them. You get the picture. It's a really good story with all sorts
of spooky elements, but there are so many versions, retold so
many times over the past century and a half, that nobody has
any idea how the real story goes.

So here's what I'd recommend. If you have an hour to kill,
perhaps you could go to Bucksport and stand in front of the
Buck grave staring at the murky image with an air of wonder-
ment and mystical detachment. Dollars to doughnuts somebody
(preferably a young, gullible local child) will wander by while
you're there and ask what you're looking at. At that point, you
can just make up your own version of the story using some
mix-and-match combination of the above-mentioned characters.
This could be fun. It just goes to show that you don't have to be
Stephen King to create a famous Maine ghost story. If your version contains even a smattering of the standard elements, it
will merge effortlessly with all the rest of the tales floating

around, and you'll have the satisfaction of knowing that you've contributed to the great Maine storytelling tradition.

All I ask is that you treat Jonathan Buck sympathetically. His only crime seems to have been living and dying before this whole story ever got started.

## ROAD MARKERS TO CALAIS
### Calais

We're all used to the mile markers on the Maine Turnpike and Route 95. In the old days we used to measure our distance by the number of miles the billboard told us we were from Perry's Tropical Nut House in Belfast. But even before that, there were road markers, placed by a wealthy Mainer, on a stretch of what is now Route 1 outside Calais.

According to the *Bangor Daily News,* these twelve granite markers were set by James Shepherd Pike to measure the distance between his mansion in Robbinston and his office in Calais. Before odometers were in use, Pike needed a means to measure the miles. According to the article, "He tied a rag around the spoke of a carriage wheel and had a man count every time that rag came up, and as he knew the diameter of the wheel, he knew when a mile was passed, and had the place marked and a stone set up." This was probably some time in the 1870s, after Pike had served a stint as ambassador to The Hague.

Pike used the mile distances to measure the performance of his horses—a sort of early time trial. The original stones have remained, except for mile 6, which is made from red granite, unlike the others, which are gray. The markers are listed on the National Register of Historic Places.

# DICK CURLESS, COUNTRY LEGEND

I wouldn't call Dick Curless a "quirky" character, but I'd call him a character out of the Maine mold. Here was a man from the very top of the country who made it to the top of the country charts.

Born in Fort Fairfield, Dick Curless first used his vocal powers as a disc jockey, here in New England and later on Armed Forces Radio during the Korean War, where he was known as "the Rice Paddy Ranger." His experience was the basis for his song "China Nights," according to his friend Al Hawkes.

Dick recorded some 78 rpm records in his early days. "They don't sound like the Dick Curless we think of now," says Al, "because his voice hadn't fully developed." After returning from the war, Al recorded some of Dick's early songs, including "The Streets of Laredo" and "The Foggy, Foggy Dew." And although he is now remembered for his beautiful bass/baritone voice, Al said that Dick Curless had a terrific vocal range, including a wonderful falsetto. Dick Curless singing falsetto is sort of like Marshall Dodge, the Maine humorist, talking with a New Jersey accent—you wouldn't really expect it.

Dick developed his fame by appearing on Arthur Godfrey's national television show in 1957. His big song was "Nine-Pound Hammer." One version of the song was recorded in Westbrook, featuring a fifteen-year-old Lenny Breau on guitar (Breau later had a meteoric career in Nashville). Al Hawkes says that when Dick was recording the part about the gas in the coal mine, Lenny Breau either moved in his chair or released his own gas, which made the next six takes of the song impossible.

According to Al Hawkes, Dick could have been a star after he appeared on the Godfrey show. "A manager wanted him to play some clubs in New Jersey and get him ready for the big-time stage. But Dick had an oral contract to play at a joint in Bangor with a sawdust floor, so he went and did that instead."

After some success, Dick toured with Buck Owens and appeared in Branson, Missouri, and Nashville.

The big hit for Dick Curless was the truckin' anthem "Tombstone Every Mile." We Mainers were proud of that song. There are millions of songs about the heat of the South and the Mexican border; but this song is from our country, where the Haynesville Road is just "a ribbon of ice." It spoke of the hard lives of the everyday working people in the northern part of Maine and the risks they take just to make a living. This ain't no "Achy Breaky Heart"—this is the real thing, real country music. The song went near the top of the country charts in the 1960s.

There were two Maine-related men who had eye patches in the 1960s. One was the "Hathaway shirt man," whose patch was a symbol, an advertising gimmick, for the shirts produced in Waterville, Maine. The other was Dick Curless. His patch was worn because of an eye problem he had from birth, according to Al Hawkes. Like the man and his songs, it was the real thing.

Some of Dick's other hit songs were "All of Me Belongs to You," "Big Wheel Cannonball," and "Baby, Baby," which is still being played locally. "You didn't bring the songs to Dick. He'd bring them to you and would play what he liked," says Al Hawkes. "Of course, that was different when he went with a big label."

Dick Curless died too young at age sixty-three. They replaced the Haynesville Road with Route 95, which has a lot fewer tombstones. But his spirit is still there in the heart of every trucker who brings the spuds down from the county in the wintertime, knowing that you can "count 'em off. There'd be a tombstone every mile."

*D U D   R O C K W E L L :*
*K E E P E R   O F   T H E   W Y E T H   F L A M E*
*Cushing*

**C**hristina's World by Andrew Wyeth, one of the most
universally recognized and admired paintings of all time,
was created in Cushing, Maine, just a few minutes' drive
off busy Route 1 near Thomaston. The building visible in the
background, a weathered Maine farmhouse, family home of
Christina and Alvaro Olsen, would be recognized at a glance by
millions. So it's no wonder that a steady stream of art lovers and
curiosity seekers make the pilgrimage to Cushing each year to
gawk at the famous structure.

The Olsen House is still there alright, standing in the middle
of a field, looking eerily similar to the way it looked the day
Wyeth first painted it half a century ago. Also still standing,
looking almost as weatherbeaten, yet amazingly fit and spry for
his eighty-eight years, is Dudley "Dud" Rockwell. Every weekday
during tourist season (Memorial Day through Columbus Day) at
2:00 P.M. sharp, Dud gives a tour of the Olsen House, complete
with anecdotes about the former occupants and what seems to be
an awful lot of casual inside information about the famous
painter himself. How does he know all this stuff, anyway?

Despite being notoriously fond of his pipe, Dud's not blowing smoke when it comes to the Wyeths. As a matter of fact,
Dudley Rockwell is about as close to being a Wyeth as you can
get without benefit of DNA. "There was three of them James
girls around here," he explains. "Louise was the oldest, then
there was Gwen, and the youngest was Betsy. I married the oldest one, and Andy married the youngest." Ayuh, you got it.
Dud's Andrew Wyeth's brother-in-law. And it doesn't take long
to figure out that he loves his "work." According to Dud, "If I

*Dud's part of the landscape around here.*

didn't do it, I'd be dead. I'm eighty-eight now and it's the only thing that keeps me going."

The Wyeths—father N.C., son Andrew, and grandson Jamie—are the closest thing to a dynasty the American art world has ever produced. Their fame has bred an understandable level of Kennedy-like reclusiveness, which in turn has bred an almost insatiable curiosity among their many admirers. Dud isn't revealing any family secrets on this tour. But he manages to give visitors a peek behind the curtain, a glimpse of the personal world of the Wyeths that most folks never see.

Far from being a mere Wyeth sycophant or a stagehand in their play, Dud's actually an incredibly interesting and talented man in his own right. His ship models are on display at the house, and the furnishings include Dudley's lovingly and expertly handcrafted replica of Alvaro's chair, made famous by one of Andrew's paintings.

And he's not a bit shy about inserting his own illustrious family background into the monologue if he senses his audience is getting restless. This has happened a few times. "A couple will come in," says Dud, "and usually it's the wife who is interested in the Wyeths." When that happens, he has a surefire technique to get hubby to sit up and take notice. "Did you ever hear of the Rockwell hardness tester?" he asks. That's clearly a change up pitch, and Dud says it usually works. A lot of them have heard of it and start asking questions. In case you are poorly informed, I'll fill you in. According to Dud, the famous Rockwell hardness tester, a device used to test the hardness of metals, was invented by his father, Stanley P. Rockwell, back in the 1920s and has been used and appreciated in metal manufacturing operations around the globe ever since—presumably by married guys with art-loving wives who wouldn't know *Christina's World* from a velvet Elvis.

## MAINE DESIGNER JEANS: FLASH 'EM THE DEER ISLE SMILE
### Deer Isle

It seems like everybody is a clothing designer these days. When I was a kid, there were only a couple of name brands sewn on the back pocket of what were then called dungarees. Nowadays all you need is a few million bucks from the sale of your latest CD, and suddenly you're a "designer" cranking out stylish (or at least wicked baggy) denim creations that will be sucked up by mall rats as soon as they hit the shelves.

Mainers (Maine workingmen mostly) have been on the cutting edge, or at least the drooping edge, of haute couture for years. If you think this business of wearing blue jeans halfway down your butt is some new trend from New York or L.A., you must not have spent much time gazing out across the clam flats of Maine over the past several decades.

Call it Maine pride, but I think it's high time we give credit for fashion innovation where credit is due. Long before the mall rats and rap artists were doing it, Maine clam diggers had perfected the technique of wearing a pair of blue jeans in such a way as to expose large portions of their backsides to the motoring public along coastal Route 1.

These guys aren't sissies, either. They work hard bent over a clam hoe all day, and they want you to know it. You won't find any of this fashion-conscious nonsense where the undershorts are hiked up around the navel while the pants waist hovers halfway to the knee. No, sir.

You get a good gawk at a Maine clam digger's backside, and you'll see the real deal in the flesh, nothing to block your view of the gloriously upraised posterior, hung out for all (especially out-of-state rusticators) to view in all of its unadorned natural splendor.

They even have a name for it. When you see a clam digger thus clad, we hope you won't take offense. He's just flashin' you the "Deer Isle Smile."

## WERU RADIO
### *Ellsworth*

*O*ne of the most interesting attractions on the roadways of Maine can't be found by looking out the windshield or poring over a map. To experience the original eclectic quirkiness of this one, you need look no further than the dashboard of your car. If you're driving along the coast between Damariscotta and Cherryfield and as far inland as Route 95, just reach out and tune your FM dial to 89.9 and check out WERU (get it?) community radio. Station manager Matt Murphy refers to WERU as "listener supported and volunteer powered." Volunteer powered? That's right. This is a 15,000-watt station

*Maine's famous for fresh air and nice waves. WERU radio is*
*famous for nice, fresh Maine airwaves.*

with over sixty "I'm just doing this because I dig it" volunteers.
Folks host shows at all hours of the day and night. Believe me,
that makes for some darn interesting programming.

A lot of what goes out over the airways on WERU simply
can't be heard anywhere else on the planet. Although the station owns a vast and varied music library (over 25,000 titles
and growing), the volunteers are just as apt to lug in their own
stuff from home. Where else are you going to hear a show
called "Talking Furniture" (a reference to the days of massive
Philcos and Motorolas in the middle of the living room), where
host "Rass Chicopee" turns you on to his own unlikely mix of
reggae, salsa, jazz, and polka? Strange musical bedfellows
indeed, but it makes you want to keep listening if only to find
out what he's going to play next. Or tune in some night when a
local middle school teacher transforms herself into the mysterious "Paula Greatorex" and hosts her own show, "Blues, the
Healer."

WERU is to off-the-wall programming what Rush Limbaugh is to right-wing political bombast. What it boils down to is that when your neighbors are running the station, you just never know what will happen next. That's really the whole point of WERU. You just gotta tune in and find out.

### WILBUR THE LOBSTER:
### THE CRUSTACEAN IS IN
#### *Ellsworth*

Unsuspecting travelers cruising along Route 1 5 miles east of Ellsworth in Hancock may be startled at the sight of a huge flaming red crustacean making its way toward an old-fashioned brick open-air lobster cooker. "Wilbur the Lobster," as he has been dubbed by Ruth and Wimpy, the owners of the eatery that bears their name, has a decidedly muscle-bound look to him. If Arnold Schwarzenegger were ever reincarnated as a lobster, he'd look like this guy. It's not clear at first glance whether Wilbur is acting out a primal death wish as he crawls toward the steaming cooker or just heading for a soak in the hot tub after pumping iron in the Arachnid Gym. Either way, he's a traffic stopper, and in the tourist business that's all that counts. According to Wimpy, the monumental sculpture, a creation of local sculptor Joe Rizzo, has been a "huge" hit ever since he first crawled into their parking lot back in 1995.

Besides turning out a menu that features over one hundred homemade items, local entrepreneurs Ruth and Wimpy (he picked up the nickname in childhood from Popeye's hamburger-gulping pal on Saturday morning cartoons) obviously have a lot of fun with the folks who stop in. According to the couple, there's no doubt that Wilbur has been good for business. So many people stop and have their pictures taken with Wilbur that the local one-hour photo developer lives in a more or less perpetual state of déjà vu.

*Is this the "real" Wilbur the Lobster?*
*Better check inside to make sure.*

Fortunately, after a photo op a lot of them decide to stay for lunch or dinner, and many become regular customers, bringing their friends and family back next summer. So everybody's happy, huh?

"Well," said Wimpy, "there are some folks who get kind of upset."

"Upset about what?" I asked.

"Our sign and the postcards and so forth all say 'Ruth and Wimpy's—Home of Wilbur the Lobster.' "

"And?" I queried.

"I hate to say this," said Wimpy, "but some folks are disappointed when they come inside. They're expecting to find a live 7½-foot lobster waiting there."

Oh, I get it: "Home of Wilbur the Lobster." Where's the real Wilbur? Hey, what are ya gonna do? You give 'em a giant fiberglass lobster, and they want a live one. I guess you just can't please some people. As I was finishing up, I thought to ask Ruth and Wimpy what their last name is. "Wilbur," he said proudly. Somehow I should have known that.

## CHESTER GREENWOOD, EAR PROTECTOR
### *Farmington*

I n most towns, the big celebration is some time in the summer, when the crowds can gather outdoors in the warm weather. Not so in Farmington, where the first day of winter marks the celebration of Chester Greenwood Day. Chester Greenwood (1858–1937) was the renowned inventor of the earmuff, so winter is an appropriate time to celebrate. (Of course, if everyone wears earmuffs, it does make it hard to hear the band.)

Chester Greenwood invented his first pair of "ear protectors" at age fifteen, and he had patented the device by the time he was eighteen. He made the first pair with some pliers and coverings and linings sewed by his grandmother. Ten years later, he developed a spring-and-steel hinge, as well as machinery to manufacture the earmuffs; he continued his improvements so that the protectors could be folded to a compact size.

In 1883, the Chester Greenwood Company sold 30,000 pairs of ear protectors; by 1918, the figure had risen to 216,000, and by 1936, 400,000 were shipped out. The first muffs were all black velvet, but by 1932, there were brighter colors, including checks and plaids.

Chester demonstrated both his product and the process of manufacturing it at the state fair in Lewiston in 1880; he received a medal for his exhibit.

Even without the earmuffs, Chester is recognized for some of his inventive and entrepreneurial accomplishments. In the late 1890s, he started the Franklin Telephone & Telegraph Company, and he manufactured all of the equipment. (An early telephone conversation: "Hello?" "What?" "Will you take off those earmuffs so you can hear what I'm saying?" "WHAT?") Chester also invented or developed a cotton picker (not much use for one in Franklin County), a "teakettle reinforcement," and a doughnut hook. His patented tempered steel rake sold in great quantities in the late 1930s. His company developed machinery so that other companies could make stuff like rolling pins and tool handles. Believe it or not, Chester also designed and manufactured a better mousetrap, which was in demand by local hotels and inns.

His biography notes that he regularly ran a mile without becoming out of breath, that he was a teetotaler, and that he was a regular member of the Odd Fellows.

So bring on the bands, even though there's snow in the streets, and even though we can't hear the notes because our earmuffs are in place. Let's warm our ears in honor of the man from Farmington, Chester Greenwood.

## SAND? YOU LOOKIN' FOR SAND? STEP RIGHT UP!
### Freeport

If you should begin to tire of the lovely green landscape and the rockbound coast and you find yourself hankering for a change of pace, I might be able to offer some assistance. As a matter of fact, if you're anywhere near Freeport when boredom strikes, I've got just the spot for you.

There are two names for this roadside attraction. Mostly, over the years, folks have referred to it as the Desert of Maine. The more mundane (but probably more technically accurate) name, sometimes used in advertising, is the Old Sand Farm. When I was a kid (back in the prehighway beautification era, when billboards ruled the earth), there were some pretty eye-catching signs around for this peculiar roadside attraction. Mostly, as I recall, they featured a parched-looking camel, a boiling tropical sun, and a palm tree or two—not exactly lobsters and lighthouses. Actually, those signs bore more than a passing resemblance to the picture on the Camel cigarette pack. At least the artist who painted the billboards had the restraint to lose the pyramids in his version.

So how did a desert end up in the state of Maine, anyway? Interestingly enough, geologists theorize that the acres of fine beachlike sand arrived about the same time, and via the same natural delivery system, as Maine's famous rocky coast. Ayuh, when all else fails, blame it on a glacier.

This unique geological phenomenon was discovered (uncovered?) back in 1797, when the acreage was purchased by a farmer named William Tuttle. Frankly, I can't imagine Tuttle being all that thrilled to realize that, despite his best efforts, all his topsoil kept blowing away, revealing hundreds of acres of sand just underneath it. I mean, c'mon, farming in Maine in the eighteenth century was hard enough already. Eventually he gave up, and the farm was purchased by a fellow named Goldrup. Rather than fight the elements, Goldrup did what hundreds of other enterprising Americans have done with their oddities and curiosities: He put up a sign and started charging people to come and gawk. It must have been a pretty good idea. He did that for sixty-five years, and the Desert of Maine is still drawing 'em.

Now, folks visiting Maine in the summer have been known to gripe about the relative dearth of sand beaches. If you run into any, just tell 'em if they're hankerin' for sand, you know just where to look.

# LOBSTER BOAT RACING

The Maine lobsterman, like his western counterpart, the working cowboy, is a legendary American figure. He is, in many ways, a throwback to an earlier, simpler time, almost a mythical figure—the tough, independent workingman who routinely risks life and limb to wrest a living from a temperamental and frequently hostile environment.

To make a living at it, a lobsterman must be a combination of expert seaman, naturalist, weatherman, mechanic, engineer, and entrepreneur. It also helps if you have an independent streak as wide as the New Jersey turnpike, a body that can pump iron all day on a couple of baloney sandwiches and a thermos of coffee, a sense of humor, and a strong, competitive spirit. It's all of that stuff, especially the competitive spirit, that makes the Maine lobster boat races such a blast.

Men like Clive Farrin and Billy Hallinan, both from my hometown of Boothbay Harbor, are typical lobster boat racers. They're hardworking lobstermen year-round. But, like the legendary "thunder road" moonshiners who became the founding fathers of NASCAR stock car racing, what these fellas really like to do is make their boats go FAST! Once they've done that, they can tinker around with 'em, modify a propeller here, tweak a fuel system there, throw in a hotter camshaft, and make 'em go FASTER!!

While there are certainly purpose-built rigs out there, boats that go racing but never haul a trap, these are looked upon with disdain on the working waterfront. No, the point here isn't to have some hot-rodded rig that's too temperamental for the real world. The big challenge, the one that gets men like Billy and Clive all worked up, is to own and operate a boat that gets you where you need to go safely and reliably, fishes 600 traps, day in and day out, fair weather or foul, then proceeds to scream like a banshee, skim across the swells, and basically blow off all comers on the weekends.

There are eight major lobster boat races in Maine. The first is in Boothbay Harbor, followed by Jonesport/Beals Island, Stonington, Harpswell, Friendship, Winter Harbor, Pemaquid, and Searsport, in that order. According to Farrin, the whole Maine lobster boat racing scene started back in the 1950s on Mossebec Reach, the long, narrow body of water that separates the seaside village of Jonesport from nearby Beals Island. The Jonesport/Beals race is still held annually on Fourth of July weekend. There are a dizzying array of classes to keep track of, from outboard-powered open boats under 16 feet all the way up to the "unlimited class," with working lobster boats in excess of 40 feet whose highly modified engines regularly crank out 700 to 800 horsepower.

Perhaps you think that the whole process has gotten too professional. Well, consider this. After endless hours of preparation and thousands of dollars spent on modifications, this is what lobster boat racing really boils down to: The winner of the unlimited class at Jonesport/Beals, arguably the race of the season, walks away with a modest prize package including such coveted items as a case of motor oil and a year's subscription to the Coastal Fisheries News. That's it. With a cash value of maybe a couple hundred bucks in a good year, that's not what these men are after. In addition to the prizes, though, there is something far more important at stake. What keeps these fellas dreaming and scheming and turning wrenches all through the long Maine winter is just this: bragging rights. Ayuh, in the end, it all comes down to which of these men will be able to get up at the crack of dawn, slug down a cup of coffee, and head out to spend the day at the helm of "the world's fastest lobster boat." Perhaps you think that's a bit overblown. I mean, "the world's fastest"? Of course, if you'd like to discuss this with the winner, you have a perfect right to do so. Just let me know ahead of time, OK? I'd like to be there to hear the conversation.

If you were expecting a little leisurely sightseeing, you picked the wrong boat!

## FREEPORT BIG INDIAN (FBI)
### Freeport

The FBI, or BFI (in polite company, the F is for "Freeport"), stands about 40 feet high and overlooks the highway coming from Yarmouth toward Freeport. Sources vary as to when he started his vigil, but most people recall his arriving some time after the 1950s. At that time, the Indian looked down on a very busy two-lane Route 1; now there are four more lanes of Route 95 whizzing by.

When he arrived in town, from Pennsylvania via the New Jersey turnpike, the Indian attracted a lot of attention. Many people paused just to have their picture taken with him, then stopped in at the Casco Bay Trading Post for a souvenir. This was a store that sold moccasins, duck decoys, balsam pillows, and Indian bead belts that smelled like skunks.

After the trading post folded, there was an engine repair shop, and a clothing store at the site. The advertising for the clothing store was simple: Just look for the Big Freeport Indian.

Built of steel rods, fiberglass, and plywood, the statue probably weighs more than a ton. No doubt the view from the top of his headdress would include the harbor at South Freeport.

Those in the more politically correct crowd don't call him the FBI anymore. Instead, he's the MBNA—Maine's Big Native American. Some people think he's a Passamaquoddy, but they could never explain how a sculptor from Pennsylvania would know how to carve a Passamaquoddy Indian. If you're driving through Freeport, take Route 1 for a change, and stop and say "hello."

*Is it just me or does this fellow seem like he'd be happier somewhere a bit to the west of Freeport, Maine?*

## JULES VITALI,
## THE FATHER OF "STYROGAMI"
### Freeport

**M**illions of people all over America (you're very likely one of them) carry the graphic art of Jules Vitali around with them every day. Jules figures that reproductions of his designs are so common that they are very possibly "second only to paper money" in terms of the number of copies floating around out there. So how come you've never heard of this talented artist, when the sheer volume of reproductions of his work dwarfs that of all three Wyeths put together? And where can you find his stuff, anyway?

Well, for starters, try your wallet or purse or wherever else you carry your identification. You see, for the past twenty-three years Jules Vitali has been working for Polaroid Corporation expressing his creative spirit by designing driver's licenses.

The truth is, even creative geniuses sometimes gotta have a day job. But, after toiling nearly a quarter century in the corporate fields, Jules recently decided he just had to break out and give full expression to his creativity. It turns out that while cranking out those driver's licenses Mr. Vitali had been secretly developing the revolutionary art form he calls "styrogami." What's styrogami? Well, it looks like delicate origami, only it's painstakingly hand-carved from a humble Styrofoam cup.

According to Jules, "I acquired an interest in Styrofoam as a medium about nineteen years ago, ironically while sipping coffee out of a cup made from same. I carry a razor-sharp jackknife called a 'peanut.' " Jules proceeded to carve the empty cup into an intricate and unique pattern, and the first piece of styrogami was born. "I've amassed over a thousand of these pieces," he explains, "each of which is as unique as a fingerprint. I carve only one or

*Picasso in Styrofoam?*

two per week, which extrapolated over a period of years, threatened to overrun my garage."

Perhaps it was simply the need to park his car indoors during the long Maine winter that finally gave Jules Vitali the motivation to break out of his safe corporate niche and head for the top of the art world. But the results have been very satisfying. He's had several shows, has more lined up, and has even experimented with casting some of his fabulous delicate creations in brass and precious metals. At any rate, he's sure having fun, and people really like his new work, even if they aren't as likely to show it to state troopers as often as they would his earlier work. While other mediums are subject to degradation over the years, Vitali feels that, although delicate, his work will stand the test of time. "People tend to see stars, crowns, snowflakes, spaceships, and various other forms upon initial viewing," says the artist. "Children love them." Besides, "Life is short, Styrofoam is long."

## L.L. BEAN:
## "START HERE. . . . COME FULL CIRCLE!"
### Freeport

The L.L. Bean retail store in Freeport is undeniably a mecca, perhaps even *the* mecca of American retail marketing. A veritable shrine to hard work and honest value, "Bean's," as it has come to be known, is open twenty-four hours a day, seven days a week, fifty-two weeks a year. The L.L. Bean mystique draws hundreds of thousands of shoppers annually, and for good reason. High-quality innovative products like the classic Maine Hunting Shoe, backed by a no-questions-asked, money-back-if-you're-not-satisfied policy, have proven to be firm bedrock for a vast retail empire. Over the years the locals have watched in awe as the fame and success of this quintessentially Maine company grew.

We also watched in awe (and perhaps a bit of alarm) as the simple wood frame store in Freeport grew and grew. Of course, success breeds success, and L.L. Bean is nothing if not successful. So, pretty soon the original old wooden building on Main Street in Freeport was replaced by a much larger and more imposing one built of stone and metal (featuring an indoor pond stocked with brook trout). Inevitably, as floor space increased, "green space" outside the structure decreased, until nearly every inch of the surrounding acreage had been paved to provide parking for the increasing tide of eager shoppers.

How ironic is that? Here's a company whose whole success rests on appreciation and preservation of nature, wilderness, and the outdoors, and there's hardly a blade of grass within walking distance of the place.

*The modest beginnings of a legendary retail store.*

That all changed in the summer of 1999, when L.L. Bean held a grand opening for its latest addition. Yup, right in the middle of what seems like endless acres of free parking, there is now a "green space." That's right. Hey, they ripped up the pavement and replaced it with grass and trees and natural shade . . . right there where grass and trees and natural shade had been in the first place. L.L. Bean advertising features the slogan "Start Here . . . Go Anywhere!" In this case, perhaps the line should read "Start Here . . . Come Full Circle!"

## A-1 DINER
### Gardiner

You could walk into the A-1 Diner in Gardiner, and order a cheeseburger and fries or a plate of fried haddock. The question is: Why would you when the menu includes such gourmet delights as Thai crab stew, mushroom risotto, and roasted garlic penne?

Why settle for liver and onions when you could be savoring the squash and apple bisque?

From the street, the A-1 looks just like any other classic American diner. You can still find these scattered around the country. Built in Worcester, Massachusetts, back in the 1940s, the A-1 has that lovely "railroad car" look with its art deco wood and stainless steel interior. But, as is so often the case in the state of Maine, there's more here than meets the eye.

*Sure, you can get a ham sandwich here.*
*But, why would you?*

The A-1 has been an institution in Gardiner for decades, and for the first forty years or so the menu didn't change any more than the decor. But when Michael Giberson bought the place from his father back in the late '80s, he figured it was time to shake things up a bit. After many years spent honing his culinary talents in restaurant kitchens from New York to L.A., Michael had collected plenty of exotic recipes to try out on his customers. How about some tofu, red pepper, and cashew curry, or a plate of spicy Basque chicken paella? If you haven't tried the Vietnamese bouillabaisse, you just aren't keeping up. The menu gets more ambitious each year. Of course, if you prefer a glass of chardonnay to a cup o' joe, Michael will be pleased to accommodate you.

If you're concerned that things might be getting too nouveau and chichi down at the old diner, you'll be happy to know that seventy-three-year-old Bob Newel is still back there in the kitchen, cranking out basic diner chow—homemade biscuits, pancakes, gravy, and salad dressings—just as he has been for the past forty-eight years. Waitress Cindy Delong, another character right out of central casting, has been taking orders and bantering with her regulars for four decades. According to Michael, she's a real class act. She'll remember your name, how you like your coffee, and presumably whether you'd prefer a plate of ham and eggs or the poached salmon with lemon butter sauce.

## *Lisa's Lobster: What a View!*
### *Georgetown*

**B**esides fresh caught lobsters right on the wharf, Lisa's Lobster on Georgetown Island, offers tourists and natives alike a true "slice of Maine life" experience. For starters, just finding the place is a real "you can't get there from here"

*Are we there yet?*

proposition. Located only a few miles off Route 1, part of the "charm" of Lisa's is the trek you have to make to find it.

First you take the Georgetown Road, also known as the Five Islands Road (if you're gonna get really picky about details, it's Route 127 south), which diverges from Route 1. Just as you cross the Bath Bridge headed north (or just before you cross the bridge headed south . . . you with me so far?), drive down the road about 7 or 8 miles and, after you've crossed the third bridge, start looking for little hand-painted signs tacked up on pine trees by the side of the road. The first one I saw read LISA'S LOBSTER 7 MILES, or so I thought. The clearly amateur sign painter had painted a tiny black dot just before the 7. To confuse things a bit more, the next sign (a half mile closer) indicates that you've got another mile to go. At least the arrows point in the right direction.

As you get closer to Lisa's, the signs get more encouraging (KEEP GOING . . . YOU'RE ALMOST AT LISA'S) at about the same time the road conditions begin to deteriorate. The tar turns to rutted dirt and the scenery starts running heavily to rusted cars, cultch-enshrouded trailers, and abandoned satellite dishes. Forget about "the way life should be"; a trip to Lisa's affords you a good gawk at the way life really is. But perseverance pays off, and before you know it, clotheslines strung from rusted Subaru carcasses give way to as charming a seaside picnic spot as you'll find on the Maine coast. And, once you get there, you can select from a menu that includes boiled lobsters, steamed and fried clams, fried scallops, fried shrimp, fried haddock, burgers, hot dogs, and french fries.

Lisa Crosby, a bouncy, energetic twenty-one-year-old entrepreneur, opened the place in the summer of '98 when she was still a senior in high school. She's been doing a land-office business ever since. She takes a philosophical view of the eyesore-laden approach to her establishment. "If they're gonna find me, they're gonna find me," she shrugs. "If not, they're gonna go somewhere else." What, and miss all this great scenery? Perish the thought!

*Lisa's . . . "delight at the end of the road."*

### RANDY SPENCER:
## THE SINGING MAINE GUIDE
#### Grand Lake Stream

**A**t this point in his career, it seems almost cruel to point
out that Randy Spencer, a registered Maine guide (don't
mess around with those unregistered ones, OK?), is
actually "from away" (he was born in Willimantic, Connecticut,
back in 1948). Despite this unfortunate accident of birth, you'd
be hard-pressed to find a stronger, or more vocal, advocate for
the glories of life in the Maine North Woods than Randy. He
points out that his love affair with Maine began with his first
visit when he was a year old and has only deepened since.

Spencer's love of Maine is matched only by his love of music.
Just out of college, back in 1971, he grabbed his backpack and
guitar and hitched his way around Europe, paying his way with
tips tossed into his open guitar case on the streets of Athens and
Rome. But the bright lights and sophistication of Europe just
couldn't compete with a flickering campfire and the rustic
simplicity of his favorite spot on earth, tiny Grand Lake Stream,
Maine.

It was while guiding out-of-state "sports" to secret fishin'
holes deep in the Maine wilderness that Randy Spencer wrote
his "big hit" song. Big hit? You bet! According to Randy, in 1975
his ditty went all the way to number 1 on radio stations located
"all over northern Maine, eastern Maine, and Maritime Canada."
The song that brought him stardom? Need you ask? It's called
"Black Flies!" a bluesy, gritty acoustic number with the refrain
"Blackflies, in your hair and in your eyes! In the old North
Woods don'tcha be surprised, when you meet those devils in

*Maine's own Backwoods Balladeer of the Blackfly.*

disguise!" The song goes on to describe these pint-size demons with an emotional intensity born of intimate knowledge of his subject matter. The radio airplay led to a tour of "some of the high places and *all* of the low ones," according to Randy. While you probably won't be seeing Randy Spencer, the singing Maine guide, on MTV anytime soon, he's not complaining. After more than a half century that little boy from Connecticut has grown up into a genuine legend of the Maine North Woods.

## *GRAVE OF THE UNKNOWN CONFEDERATE SOLDIER*
### *Gray*

What can be said about a town named Gray? It is home to the Gray Water District. (Do you really want to drink "gray water"?) It has a Gray Marketplace, not quite a black market, and news items from the town are deemed "Gray Matters."

Perhaps the answer can be found at the Gray Historical Society, on the second floor of the former Pennell Institute. The society's museum features cases of memorabilia from the town, which was incorporated in 1778. It is hosted by active volunteers, Gray ladies, who are anxious to tell the historical legends of the town. One volunteer solemnly stated, "Gray has a colorful history."

Gray is the location of the first woolen mill in the United States. It was a central spot on the Portland–Lewiston Interurban Railroad (some of the rights-of-way from this road run through the fields and forests of Gray). And there is a remnant of the Civil War, located right in the center of town.

In the Civil War, Gray sent 200 of its sons into action; the Historical Society claims this was the most from any town in the state. Many boys did not come back alive, including one Lieutenant Colley. His family sent for his body, but when the casket arrived, it contained the remains of an unknown man clad in the uniform of a Confederate soldier. The uniform was, of course, gray. No one knows why this body clad in gray was sent to the town of Gray. And no one knows for certain whether the man really was a Confederate soldier or if a captured Confederate uniform was used to wrap the body.

The unknown soldier was buried in an unmarked plot in the Gray Cemetery. Lieutenant Colley's body came home and was buried nearby. Gray ladies, and the Colley family, arranged for a

*The Civil War Monument in Gray. Does it make a Reb "blue" to be buried in Gray? Whose side was this guy on anyway?*

stone to be set up for the unfortunate Reb. It's still there, marked "stranger." In an old black-and-white photo, the grave is adorned by an American flag. Today, on Memorial Day, the grave has two Confederate flags, donated by the Daughters of the Confederacy. The grave, in Lane H of the Gray Cemetery, is something of a shrine for southern sympathizers. Confederate reenactors encamp near the site, which is some 1,000 miles north of the northernmost Civil War battle site. Gray merchants probably don't sing the blues about the influx of gray soldiers bringing their greenbacks.

There's another Civil War memory in Gray. The heroic monument, built in 1911 and formerly located at one end of town, was recently moved to improve traffic circulation, to a spot closer to the cemetery, at the intersection of Routes 26 and 100. To an untrained eye, the soldier on this monument also looks like a southerner—maybe it's the hat. But the Gray ladies of the Historical Society say this monument is one of many similar stone soldiers built by a firm in Auburn and still to be found in northern New England towns.

The red, white, and blue, and the stars and bars—long may they wave o'er the green fields of Gray.

## GET NAKED IN MAINE!
### Gray

Get naked in Maine! Don't you just get goose pimples thinking about it? For several years in the middle of the twentieth century, sun worshipers flocked to the flesh capital of the state, Gray, to revel in their altogethers. No one I spoke to remembers much about it. One woman said her doctor treated someone there once. "For sunburn?" I asked. "The doctor didn't say," she said.

*You were expecting a picture of a nudist? Take a really close look. See?*
*Right there in the upper left-hand corner.*

People did know where the nudist camp had been, on Cotton
Road. Today, Cotton Road doesn't even exist. It's right near the
Maine turnpike. *That* would have been a scenic turnout. Maybe
the Turnpike Authority should have placed a toll plaza there.
The spot is about 2 miles south of where the highway crosses a
wildlife refuge, which is south of the game preserve. With some
additional work, the pike could have straddled the camp. What
would the road sign look like? CAUTION—NUDE FROLICKERS?

The camp went out of business many years ago. Not very
many local people attended its activities. The residents didn't
cause much trouble. According to one area historian, there was
really only one complaint: "We had a lot of low-flying aircraft in
the vicinity."

# PERCIVAL BAXTER FUN FACTS

Percival P. Baxter (1876–1969) was a monumental Mainer. Like his beloved Mount Katahdin, he was larger than life. We all know that he gave to the people of Maine the mountain and its surrounding land, to be enjoyed in its forever wild state. But you might not know the following:

1. As a young attorney, he set up a sting operation to foil a bribery effort in 1900.

2. As a student at Bowdoin College, he brought his dog, Deke, to classes with him. One time his dog vomited in class and received the sympathy of Baxter's professor.

3. While he was governor (1921–1924), the president of the Maine Central Railroad gave Baxter's dog a first-class human passenger ticket on the line.

4. When his irish setter, Garry Owen, died, Governor Baxter ordered the flags on all state office buildings to be lowered to half-staff in mourning, saying that the faithfulness of his pet stood in sharp contrast to the fickle nature of humans. Some of his dogs were buried on the grounds of the Baxter School for the Deaf, with a tombstone bigger than most stones that mark human remains.

5. In 1936, he proposed (although not publicly) that Maine secede from the United States and join Canada, and that the Kittery Bridge have a sign that read LEAVING U.S., ENTERING MAINE. Among the improvements resulting from a Maine–Canada link: "Portland would become a maritime metropolis" and "Bath would turn out ships for the British navy."

6. A bust of Baxter was placed, in 1956, in the Hall of Flags in the state house, along with war memorabilia. A state senator from the district where Baxter State Park was located tried to have the bust removed. His efforts failed, and the senator was not

reelected. The bust was damaged by a vandal in 1996. No one knew why. "If it had been [former governor John] McKernan, I would have given him a hand," one capitol observer said. As a result of a private fund-raising effort, the bust was repaired and sits, good as new, in its old location.

7. In the 1920s Baxter dedicated the Soldiers and Sailors Monument in Kittery. What no one knew was that he had hidden a letter underneath the statue, talking about public service and about his unfulfilled love life (he was never married). The letter was uncovered in the spring of 2001 during renovations to the statue. It was read by the current governor, then placed back in its container.

8. When he died, he left more money for the operation of Baxter State Park, in an effort to maintain the independence of the mountain and the park.

9. The Percival Baxter Will will be posted on the Cumberland County Registry of Probate Web site in 2002.

Besides the legacy of the splendid beauty of Katahdin, what other secrets has Percy left for us?

## *LOW-FAT TRUCKIN'*
### *Greenbush*

**H**ere's a roadside attraction most passenger vehicles don't even think about—the roadside truck scales used by the Maine state police. As reported in the *Bangor Daily News,* August 9, 2001, these scales are a matter of livelihood.

The *News* reported that several truckers received citations from the Maine state police for being overweight (not the drivers, just the vehicles) after attending a session on the state's scales. The truckers then said that, either before or after their weigh-in with the cops, they had weighed in at local mills—which paid by the pound—and they seemed to be much slimmer. In some cases, the difference was 2,900 pounds. Both the police scales and the mill scales were certified by the state. At the mills, the truckers received less money than they wanted. At the police scales, they received a fine for being overweight. One trucker called it a "double whammy."

This leads to a sort of test about one's political beliefs. There are some who think the state police are in a conspiracy to shake down the truckers, so their scales are set too high. There are others who think the police could do no wrong, but the mill owners have set their scales too low. There are still others who might say, "I don't need no set of scales. I can tell how much she weighs jest by lookin' at how low she sets."

## K EN  S NOWDEN ,  M R .  M OOSE  P OOP
### *Greenville*

**W**hat is it that makes great thinkers different from the rest of us? I figure it must be some inner vision, some quirk in the brain's wiring. There must be some spark of originality in the inner thought processes by which these folks are able to consider the normal everyday stuff that the rest of us just take for granted and see it in a whole new light. Think about it. Isaac Newton was certainly not the first guy to doze off in an orchard and get bonked on the head with an apple, right? But he was the first guy to discover the law of gravity as a result of having had that rude awakening.

Ken Snowden's discovery may not have had the same implications for the advancement of humankind as Newton's (we'll just have to wait and see on that one, won't we?), but in some ways his "moment of discovery" was not all that different.

According to Ken, the president and CEO of the aptly named Moose Poop Moosehead Lake Company, it was just an ordinary day a few years back when he was struck by inspiration. The world has never been quite the same since. It was a lovely fall day, and Snowden was more or less minding his own business, taking a walk in the woods.

Maybe he was temporarily distracted by the brilliance of the Maine autumn foliage, or perhaps, since it was hunting season, his eyes were scanning the trees for hunters who might not immediately notice that he had only two legs and was wearing a bright orange vest.

Whatever the reason, Ken's eyes were not on the trail ahead when the moment arrived. Stepping over a fallen log, his boot landed in a large, warm, soft substance. Glancing down, Ken instantly realized that he had accidentally placed his foot squarely in the center of a large, fresh pile of moose poop. I'm sure that this same experience has happened to hundreds, perhaps thousands, of outdoorsy types. Lesser men, I'm sure, have reacted to this experience with nothing more original than a string of expletives. But for Ken Snowden, standing nearly ankle deep in moose poop, the experience turned on the proverbial lightbulb. As he told me years later, "I stood there for a minute looking at my foot stuck in that stuff, and my first thought was, 'There's a market for this!' "

Striking while the iron was hot (or the boot still wet), Snowden collected a bit of the fresh dung and raced back home to his workshop to investigate the possibilities. A short while later he emerged triumphant.

Scoff all you want. I'm sure Ken is laughing, too, or at least smiling, all the way to the bank. You see, it turns out that there was indeed "a market for this." The Moose Poop Moosehead Lake Company is currently shipping moose poop earrings, tie tacks, refrigerator magnets, and a half dozen other genuine Maine moose poop products all over the country. Ken tells me that he has sold Maine moose poop jewelry throughout the South and the mid-Atlantic states. He even has customers in California. Hey, you just can't argue with success. I doubt if this stuff will ever appear in the Tiffany store on Fifth Avenue. But apparently lots of folks are eager to shell out their hard-earned cash for a chance to have their bodies adorned with the natural beauty that can only come from jewelry lovingly handcrafted from tiny chunks of authentic moose poop.

# WHAT DO YOU SAY TO A MOOSE?
## *Greenville*

When you've got lemons, you make lemonade. When you've got moose, you make . . . a tourist attraction. The Moosehead Lake Region is developing into a major moose market. Stephanie Gardiner, from the Moosehead Region Chamber of Commerce, says that eight out of ten people coming into the Chamber's office ask where they can go to see a moose. Many of these people insist that the moose are all in one spot. Some of the more zoologically challenged have asked, "When do the deer turn into moose?"

It's not uncommon for moose to wander the streets of Greenville, a la the TV show *Northern Exposure.* They are everywhere, especially on the highways at night, when they enjoy jousting with automobiles.

The region capitalizes on its moose connection. For instance there's Moosemania, a festival in early summer, which features the Tour de Moose bicycle race. One spot serves Moosehead Gingerbread. The Black Frog Restaurant serves moose balls (don't ask). Stephanie was not sure whether any restaurant served mousse for dessert.

All is not perfect in moose land, however. There are two types of people who want to see moose: those who just want to see them as part of a nature experience, and those who want to hunt them and eat them. Last year's peak foliage time coincided with the one-week moose-hunting season. As a result, several leaf peepers were looking at cars and trucks draped with dead moose. Both groups bring money into the region, but coexistence may be a problem.

This year, an effort will be made to move the hunting season ahead—the moose will always be there to shoot, but the bright colors of autumn have even shorter lives.

So what do you say to a moose? Stephanie Gardiner says, "Just leave 'em alone." Some folks in Greenville, when encountering a moose, go right up to him and whisper in his ear, "Thanks, big guy."

### *ABBOT VAUGHN MEADER:*
### *THAT'S SHOW BIZ, BUDDY*
#### *Hallowell*

**Q**uick, what's the fastest-selling recording in history? Something by The Beatles perhaps? Elvis? Alvin and the Chipmunks? You're not even close. I'll give you a hint. The album was recorded in New York City in October 1962 by a Maine man, and it sold four million copies in four weeks. How good is that? Well, consider that the previous all-time best-seller, the sound track of *My Fair Lady,* took a full year to sell that many copies. In case you haven't guessed, the record I'm referring to is *The First Family Album,* a parody of the Kennedys' White House life at the height of Camelot.

The meteoric rise and precipitous crash of Abbot Vaughn Meader's comedy career is one of the strangest and most gut-wrenching tales in show biz history. Meader, born in Waterville in 1936, was working his political comedy/parody act in New York clubs when he hit pay dirt. He was onstage, fishing for a laugh, when he ad-libbed a bit of Kennedyesque "Let me say this about that" dialogue using his native Maine accent as a basis for the universally recognized Kennedy Bahston brogue. The audience went wild.

Meader refined the skit to include other Kennedys and current political figures, and in October of 1962 (ironically on the same evening that the president went on network TV to give his "Cuban Missile Crisis" speech) he recorded his trademark parody album of the Kennedys supposed White House life. Public response to the album was huge. Sitting in a hotel room in Detroit, barely a month after the recording session, Meader began to realize the meaning of fame. In a span of a few minutes he fielded calls from the *New York Times, Life* magazine, and the *Ed Sullivan Show*. Suddenly hot as a pistol, Meader spent one dizzying year riding a rocket ship to stardom. Within twelve months the album had sold nearly eight million copies and Meader seemed destined to become one of the great comedians of the twentieth century.

But that was not to be. Where were you when you heard the news? Meader was in a taxi in Milwaukee on November 22, 1963, when the driver turned and asked, "Did you hear about the president getting shot in Dallas?" Assuming he had simply been recognized by one of his millions of fans, Meader replied, "No. How does it go?" Before the driver could explain, the radio announcer read the latest bulletin on Kennedy's assassination, and Meader's rocket ship crash-landed with a thunderous explosion. Shortly after that, comedian Lenny Bruce quipped, "They put two graves in Arlington: one for John Kennedy and one for Vaughn Meader."

Thankfully, Meader didn't die that day. But, in many ways, his career did. Despite pleas from his legions of fans, Meader has kept his vow never to resurrect the Kennedy parody act. (A grateful Bobby Kennedy wrote Meader a note thanking him for his sensitivity in volunteering to cease his JFK impression after the president's death.)

These days Meader stays mostly out of the limelight, dividing his time between his home in Florida and his home in Maine. Although he has continued to perform, notably at a restaurant in Hallowell, where Meader was the kitchen manager, and make recordings (friends and fans agree that Meader is an extremely gifted musician with a phenomenal knack for snappy, off-the-cuff parody songwriting), none of his projects has even begun to match the success of *The First Family Album*. That's probably just as well. As Vaughn Meader knows all too well, the spotlight of fame can inflict some near-fatal burns. As any fan of the Broadway musical *Camelot* (Jackie and JFK, among them) can tell you, it's a wonderfully funny, entertaining show. But the ending is a real tearjerker.

# IT'S OK TO BE "FROM AWAY"

**W**hile visiting the state of Maine, you're likely to hear quite a lot about PFAs (people "from away"). Occasionally, the comments will be mean-spirited, but that's a rarity. For the most part, the term is pretty innocuous.

So who are these folks, and why is it so important that they be identified? Well, I don't exactly know how to break this to you, but, basically, if you weren't actually born in the state, you are a PFA. PFAs fall into one of three categories:

1. *Tourists:* These are folks who stop by for only a few days, generally during the summer months.

2. *Summer People:* The old-fashioned term for these folks was "the summer complaint," but you don't hear that much these days.

3. *Transplants:* People who have moved to Maine "from away" and now live here year-round.

The biggest problem most folks have involves people in category 3. I mean, they live here year-round, right? They pay taxes here. Their kids go to school here. How come they aren't full-fledged Mainers? This is the part that bugs PFAs the most. I'll get to that in a minute.

Meanwhile, to better understand the PFA phenomenon, you'll need a little background material. Historically, Maine has pretty much always been a relatively poor, relatively isolated state (we are the only state in the nation that borders only one other state). The winters here are long and cold. The summers are marvelous, but brief. Basically, we figure it takes a certain amount of toughness to make it here over the long haul (and Mainers definitely care about the Long Haul).

On the other hand, Maine, especially in the summer, has always been a big vacation spot. But keep in mind, while all the visitors are here enjoying "Vacationland," the natives are working. After Labor Day? We're still working. In the middle of the long, dark Maine winter? Ayuh, still working, often at two or three jobs just to make ends meet (which we call "gettin' by"). So perhaps there's a little resentment at work here. The old-timers had a saying that expresses it pretty well: "If you can't take the winters, you don't deserve the summers!"

OK, maybe that explains the attitude regarding "summah folks." But what about those who do move here and stay year-round? Aren't they entitled to full native status? Well, yes and no. Actually, they are. And most of them will admit that they are not subjected to any serious discrimination and are well accepted in the community. So why are they still referred to as being "from away"? I think it's just a matter of Maine pride mixed with a big dose of traditional Yankee contrariness.

Perhaps it all boils down to the fact that, by maintaining a strict line based solely on what is generally an accident of birth (although pregnant women have been known to go to some lengths to get back to Maine so that a child can be born within the state's borders), Mainers are simply holding on tenaciously to the one thing that cannot be acquired with all the wealth, power, education, begging, wishing, hoping, or arm twisting: a Maine birth certificate.

### A CHAIN SAW MICHELANGELO
#### Hancock

**E**xamples of chain saw sculpture, typically rough-hewn bears or lobstermen or moose fashioned from great slabs of wood by chain saw wielding "artists," are fairly common in Maine. You can see them all painted up in bright primary colors in the parking lots of restaurants and gift shops or gradually acquiring a natural patina on lawns and in public parks.

Frankly, until I met Ray Murphy at his roadside chain saw sculpture emporium on Route 1 in Hancock, I just assumed that the folks who make this stuff were all pretty much alike. Boy, did he ever set me straight on that one!

*The trouble with fame is that you spend half your time
posing for pictures with fans.*

Ray Murphy is the self-proclaimed "World's Original Chain Saw Sculptor," and that's not an idle boast. According to Ray, he personally invented the art form back in 1953, when, as an eleven-year-old boy he used his chain saw to inscribe a series of four-letter words on the woodpile behind his daddy's shed.

As with all great discoveries—the wheel, electricity, the splitting of the atom—conditions had to be just right. According to Ray, the previous year "a man named Fox" had invented a new type of chain saw blade that, unlike the old-style blades, could be sharpened to an incredibly fine edge, thus allowing Ray to work in the degree of detail necessary for sculpting logs.

If you think maybe Ray is overstating his position in the chain saw sculpting hierarchy, a visit to his bus/chain saw sculpting museum, which is parked right on the lot behind the sculptures, should convince even the most hard-core skeptic. Inside the bus, a 1960 GM model with a million miles on the odometer, most of them put there by Ray himself, you will find ample evidence that he is exactly who he says he is: the World's Original (and greatest) Chain Saw Sculptor.

As proof of his claims, Ray points out that his work is currently on display in all the Ripley's Believe It or Not! museums worldwide. He is officially listed with Ripley's as the Only Man in the World who can accomplish the following seven mind-boggling feats of chain saw artistry.

Using only a standard-issue, nonmodified chain saw, Ray Murphy can

1. Carve the entire alphabet on a regular number 2 pencil.
2. Carve your name on a belt buckle while you're wearing it.
3. Carve a chair (back, seat, and four legs) out of a block of wood in ten seconds.
4. Carve a sculpture using two chain saws at the same time.
5. Carve *two* sculptures simultaneously using a chain saw in each hand.
6. Carve his name with a chain saw on the head of a wooden kitchen match without lighting the match.
7. Using only a chain saw, carve the numbers 1 through 10 on a wooden toothpick.

That last one is the topper, what Ray calls "the ultimate." He claims that this is "as near impossible as it gets" and says even he, the World's Original Chain Saw Sculptor, needs two solid weeks of intensive training before attempting it.

Ray has carved 48,471 chain saw sculptures so far, and he shows no signs of slowing down. He's a living, breathing, sawdust-blowin'-in-the-wind example of a true Maine roadside attraction.

*Come on, honey.*
*It'll look great in the den.*

## THE WASHING MACHINE IN THE TREE
### Harpswell

It isn't there anymore. It was just a bit of ephemeral found art, but I remember seeing it many times back in the early and mid-1970s, and pointing it out to everyone as we drove by it. You could see it from Route 24 coming from Brunswick and heading to Orr's Island, just after the road took a right-hand jog at Card's Cove. The road went up a hill—the old dump was somewhere near the top. And as you drove up the hill, if you looked to your left, you would see it.

It was a washing machine; I can't remember if it was wringer-style or automatic. And it was in a tree, high above the road—at least 25 to 30 feet up, balanced in the branches. I'd always be driving too fast to see if the motor was in it; frankly, I wouldn't be surprised if the motor was still there.

*Ripley's Believe It or Not* always had those articles about the corncob pipe or other man-made object that had been left so long in the branches that the tree grew around it. I was hoping, whenever I saw that machine, that the tree would muckle onto that thing and make it part of the natural surrounding.

Of course, it's not there anymore. Either some bureaucrat ordered it to come down, or it came down some night in a gale-force wind. Wouldn't that be some surprise, to see a washing machine fall out of the sky?

Like all of the other items found and seen on the roadsides of Maine (the statues, the ornaments, the signs), this item has a story. I don't know what the story is, but I'll leave it to you, the reader, to figure out or make up. I'd assume that some of the elements would include a local boy with a strong back, a moonless night, and a good quantity of Narragansett beer. You can decide whether it was hoisted in anger or in fun. And we'll all imagine the smile on the face of that fella every time he drove by his own native sculpture.

## BAILEY ISLAND BRIDGE
### *Harpswell*

**A**bout 14 miles from Cooks Corner in Brunswick is a bridge, which, because of its status as a civil engineering landmark, is listed on the National Register of Historic Places. It's the cribstone bridge that connects Orr's Island with Bailey Island on Route 24. The unique design of the bridge came about because of the way the tide works. Granite slabs were stacked in a crib, or cellular, fashion so that the tides could ebb and flow, back and forth. The slabs are strong enough to withstand the buffeting of winds and waves. At least, they have been since the late 1920s. The roadway was built on the cribs, and a sidewalk was added in 1951, according to the Department of Transportation.

# A LOVE FOR LAWN ORNAMENTS

**M**ainers take their outside decorating seriously. Some folks worry all winter as to just how they are going to place their objects in the front yard to make the appropriate statement. The art of "lawnahge" has grown through the years, and it has expanded across traditional socioeconomic strata.

Take the flamingo—please! This humble plastic bird was often the staple of lawn ornamentation. The coming of spring used to be heralded by the blooming of the pink flamingos in the window of J.J. Newberry's on Main Street. Flamingos, like most plastic lawn ornaments, had a certain charm for a certain class of people. But flamingos became the ornament of choice for the "slumming it" set. Now the plastic birds adorn Cape Elizabeth yards and professional buildings. The antiestablishment theme of lawn ornaments has been co-opted by the establishment, or at least by their yuppie children.

Here are some others:

- *Bent-over Ladies.* Now, there is an ornament lacking political correctness. You don't see many of them, mostly because the people who buy lawn ornaments are women and they'd rather not have another fat woman bent over in their yard.

- *Gazing Balls.* These are anything from high end to cheapo. The expensive ones, handcrafted and delicate, look exactly like the machine-made ones that you can get at Wal-Mart.

- *Cartoon Characters.* These will usually be found in the yards of people who also have satellite dishes, or people who spend more on their large-screen TVs than on, say, encyclopedias for the kids. The Warner Brothers cartoon characters, like Daffy Duck, Bugs Bunny, and Taz, the Tasmanian devil, are sold at every roadside ornament stand, but not, for some strange reason, at Warner Brothers stores in malls.

- *Whirligigs.* We do get a lot of wind at times here in Maine, especially in the winter. You don't need a wind-speed gauge, though, if you can see how fast the wings on your bird are a-spinning. You should never put WD40 or any kind of lubricant on the wings of whirligigs, because it might confuse them and it would give you a false idea of the wind speed.

- *Metallic Figures. These are often cut into the shape of a moose or a guy sitting there smoking a pipe. If your yard is big enough, one of these turned just right will give a driver coming down the highway a moment of thought.*

- *Exploded Tires, Painted White. Some folks think these are too "southern," since you see a lot of them when you go to Florida. Of course, the reason you see them in Florida is that someone from Maine brought them there in the first place. The tires are good for recycling, they make good planters, and they are always in good taste.*

- *Washing Machines. This is one of the best types of lawn ornaments. It takes up a lot of space, and if you have more than one on your lawn, people aren't going to bother you too much.*

Unlike a bridge over a river or a gorge, this bridge
connected the rest of the world with an isolated spot, and it had
a major impact on life. The prebridge residents of Bailey Island
were not genteel summer folk rusticating by the seashore. They
were fishermen, and the winters on an isolated island were
long. "There were a lot of Johnsons on that island," says a
member of the historical society. No doubt.

The town of Harpswell didn't want to pay for a bridge to
Bailey, but the state chipped in enough funds to build the
bridge. The bridge brought in the gift shops and summer
folks—and it put a feather in the cap of the engineers at the
State Highway Department.

## THE BUZZ THAT JUST WON'T GO AWAY
### Harpswell

**M**artinis may have been the big deal in the fabulous '50s,
but here in the twenty-first century it seems more and
more apparent that caffeine is becoming America's drug
of choice. Suddenly, there seems to be a coffeehouse on every
street corner, and people actually base their new vehicle-
purchasing decisions on the number of cup holders available per
occupant.

Brett Johnson of Harpswell is nothing if not an astute
observer of pop culture. A lifelong entrepreneur, Brett has come
up with a uniquely Maine response to the nation's seemingly
limitless thirst for strong, hot java. Brett's brew is called Maine
BlackFly Roast, and the tag line, "For the Buzz That Just Won't
Go Away," obviously gets people's attention. The stuff is "flying"
off the shelves faster than bug spray in the Allagash Wilderness.
"We sell literally tons of it to some wonderful registered Maine
guides," says Brett. And, he notes proudly, "We are the 'official
coffee' of the Maine Blackfly Breeders Association." Brett sells

Maine BlackFly Roast throughout New England, in the Adirondacks, and through mail-order catalogs as well. "L.L. Bean carries our product," says Brett, "and a great little catalog out of Glens Falls, New York, called The Pack Basket."

He even gets unsolicited fan mail attesting to the potency of his brew. The store at Mount Blue State Park serves and sells Maine BlackFly Roast. A satisfied customer e-mailed Brett extolling the virtues of the coffee with the continual kick. "After just one cup," she wrote, "I got so 'buzzed' that I cleaned the guy's store for him!"

That last one really got me thinking. If Maine BlackFly Roast really does have *that* effect on people who drink it, maybe I ought to start serving it to guests who drop by my place.

## THE "JUNQUE" MAN WITH A CURATOR'S SOUL
### *Harrington*

There are actually some world-class museums in the state of Maine; the Maine Maritime Museum in Bath and the Farnsworth in Rockland come to mind. But the Down East Museum of Natural History, located along an otherwise deserted stretch of Route 1 in the town of Harrington in rural Washington County, is in a class by itself. Class? Well, that's not exactly the first word that pops into your mind when you first clap eyes on the place. Frankly, *junkyard* would be a lot closer to the mark.

And a sprawling heap it is, too. So what's with the professionally lettered sign out front announcing to all and sundry that they've finally arrived at the Down East Museum of Natural History? Is this some sort of joke? That's what I thought, until I took the time to discuss the genesis of the "museum" with its founder, Jerry Blackburn.

Jerry moved to Maine from Sioux City, Iowa, back in 1983 and opened his roadside attraction about two years later. What it is, is "The biggest little acre in Washington County," says Jerry proudly, jammed full of "preowned" merchandise. He claims that if you take the time to paw through

*Everything you need, and a whole lotta stuff you got no use for.*

all the stuff he's got, you'd find "everything you could ever dream of . . . and mostly two or three of 'em!" The "exhibits" on display at this museum include tired fifth-hand appliances, hubcaps, kitschy living room accessories, and chipped, faded old road signs.

So the Natural History Museum sign must be just a gag, right, poking fun at rural Maine poverty? Actually and surprisingly, the answer is no. You see, it turns out that Jerry Blackburn is actually a sensitive, thoughtful guy who pays very careful attention to the stream of odds and ends that flow through the place. He may be a transplant from Iowa, but it's soon obvious he really cares about preserving every scrap of genuine Maine history he runs across. Jerry Blackburn is in fact a "junque" man with a curator's soul. For the doubters among you I offer the following evidence.

While we were talking, Mr. Blackburn fished out a section of wooden beam he had salvaged from the old Centerville schoolhouse. On the beam this poem had been penned in the careful, flowing penmanship of an earlier, simpler time:

*This is a fine frame*
*It's built with strength and might*
*It stands on a hill*
*Of beauty and delight*
*O' may it long stand tall, for the owner's good*
*And every year be filled with school days good*
*It will be a fine building*
*With plenty of room*
*May fire or tempest*
*Never it consume*

—M. D. Chandler, May 1, 1858

He's not selling that piece of history, no sir. "That," he says, "is part of the museum."

## *The Eternal Leak*
### *Houlton*

Citizens of Aroostook County are a hardy breed, not much given to complaining. They're mostly hardworking farmers making the best of the hardscrabble economy, short growing season, and long, cold Maine winter. They're well aware that the big boom in tourism that brings an annual shot of seasonal prosperity to much of the coast has long since faded to a distant echo by the time you pull into Houlton several hours north of the nearest lighthouse or lobster shack.

But, as I've said, county folks just aren't complainers. Given half a chance, they'll put the best spin on most any situation and keep on going. While they'll readily admit that most of the big tourist attractions are "down south," they don't cry over spilled milk. They just crow over spilled water . . . or leaking water . . . or whatever sort of water it is that leaks, spills, or pours twenty-four hours a day from one of Aroostook County's few genuine tourist attractions. As any schoolchild in Houlton will tell you, the attraction I'm referring to is the famous *Boy with a Leaking Boot* statue in Pierce Park at the junction of Main and Military Streets in downtown Houlton.

*How's this for a catchy slogan? "Visit Houlton, Maine! It's worth a trip . . . to watch it drip!"*

The statue, which also serves as a fresh drinking water fountain, was cast in zinc at J. W. Fiske Iron Works in New York and erected in Houlton in 1916. It depicts a young lad who has apparently just discovered a leak in his boot. Having removed the boot, he holds it aloft, a slightly bemused expression on his face, as if to say to the casual onlooker, "Oh my goodness! Look what happened! My boot has a leak in it, and it has been leaking like this ever since 1916!" That's it. No secret meaning or hidden message, no historical significance that anybody can recall. In fact, nobody in Houlton seems to know or care who the boy is or what happened to the boot or why for almost a century now it's been leaking like a sieve.

Since it's been estimated that over 10,000 photos of the Boy with the Boot statue are snapped annually, perhaps there is a message here after all, one that reflects the indomitable Aroostook spirit. Maybe the statue is saying, "Don't shy away from life's difficulties! Hold 'em right up there and take a good, long look at 'em!" If you do that long enough, who knows? Some tourists might eventually stop by to see what you're up to.

## AROOSTOOK BUMPER STICKER: NOT LIKE MASSACHUSETTS
### Houlton

Some bumper stickers only make sense, or at least make *more* sense, if you've seen another, previous bumper sticker. This is something like what happens when somebody comes along and adds a word or phrase to an existing bit of graffiti, thereby completely changing the original meaning, often with humorous results. A couple of examples of this brick wall editorializing (which humorist Jean Shepherd turned into very catchy book titles) are "Jesus Saves!" under which some wag had added the line "Moses Invests!" and the classic "In God We Trust! All Others Pay Cash!"

While visiting the Pine Tree State, you're apt to see bumper stickers, even official WELCOME TO MAINE road signs, bearing the state's most recent (and most boosterish) slogan "Maine . . . the way life should be!" If you venture north of Bangor, however (and I hope you do), you'll run across a variation on that theme. This one says: "Aroostook County, The Way Maine Used to Be." Ouch! Take that, you Swedish-car-loving, black-Lab-toting, soccer-and-mall-addicted "southern" poseurs!

Folks in "The County," viewed by many in the southern part of the state as the poor relations to the north, tend to think of Aroostook as the last bastion of pure, unadulterated Maine. Perhaps, making a virtue of necessity, County dwellers are apt to dismiss the more developed (and therefore more prosperous) southern Maine counties as being "just like Massachusetts" (a scathing invective indeed, when spoken by a native Mainer).

The "Aroostook County, The Way Maine Used to Be" bumper stickers, which began sprouting on pickup trucks and massive Buicks (the vehicles of choice in this large agricultural region) back in the mid-1990s, were the brainchild of Mr. Richard Rhoda of Houlton, a man with a seemingly bottomless well of enthusiasm for all things "County." After he came up with the slogan, Rhoda's wife had a few made up as a Christmas gift. These early examples, plastered on the family cars, generated a lot of interest and "Where can I get one?" comments.

Soon thereafter, Rhoda's son Daniel, a Houlton High School student with an entrepreneurial bent, went into business for himself selling the stickers. The rest is history. Before long you could buy them at almost any corner store in the north country. Even retail giant Wal-Mart had them flying off the shelf.

Sales of the bumper stickers peaked a couple years ago. But, you know what? That's OK. Better'n OK, actually. After all, every marketing fad runs its course sooner or later. The Rhodas had some fun with Aroostook pride, young Daniel gained some valuable business experience, and everybody got a chuckle. But, while folks in The County want to be successful,

they know that it's important not to be *too* successful. God
forbid that they ever end up accused by other Mainers of being
"just like Massachusetts."

## LISTON ON THE CANVAS, LEWISTON ON THE MAP!
### *L e w i s t o n*

I was barely thirteen years old on February 25, 1964, when a
young, brash, incredibly cocky twenty-two-year-old
prizefighter from Louisville, Kentucky, named Cassius Clay
confounded the oddsmakers and set the boxing world on its ear.
He accomplished this feat by beating world champion Sonny
Liston for the heavyweight title. My old friend and veteran TV
reporter Bill Green of WSCH-TV in Portland told me that the
fight, held in Miami, ended with a TKO for Clay in the seventh
round when Liston failed to leave his corner. According to Bill,
"Everybody wanted a rematch because few could believe it had
happened, and *nobody* liked Clay!"

So how did the rematch for the heavyweight crown end up
being held in Lewiston, Maine, of all places? "As I understand
the story, they wanted to hold the fight in Madison Square
Garden," says Bill, "There was some question as to what Liston's
real age was. Liston was the kind of a guy . . . like Mike Tyson,
that kind of a guy." Bill explained that the issue of Liston's
indeterminate age meant that New York wouldn't approve the
match. "Maine," he says, "would license Liston to fight."

Of course we would. Hey, this was big stuff for Lewiston. The
new champion, now going by the name Muhammad Ali ("though
nobody would call him that," says Bill. "They *still* didn't like
him!"), set up his training camp at the nearby Poland Spring
House. Howard Cosell and lots of other nationally known
celebrity sportscasters descended on the town. These included one
man who would achieve that status later in life: Bryant Gumbel,
then a freshman at Bates College, sold popcorn at the event.

There was a general exuberance statewide over the big event. According to Bill Green, the *Bangor Daily News* claimed to have "scooped the world" by announcing a day in advance of the fight that the bout would be refereed by "Jersey" Joe Walcott.

On the night of the fight, I stayed up pretty late and tuned in to the broadcast on my little portable AM radio. After sitting through what seemed like hours of undercard matches leading up to "The BIG EVENT! The World Heavyweight Boxing Championship, Live from Lewiston, Maine!," the big moment finally arrived. They'd even flown in a Big Broadway Star to sing the National Anthem! They couldn't have made a better choice for the mostly Franco-American Lewiston crowd than Matinee Idol Robert Goulet.

Well, looking back on it, maybe they *could* have picked a better singer . . . at least on that particular evening. I remember being perplexed that such a famous guy not only sang amazingly off-key but flat out forgot most of the lyrics to the national anthem. It came out something like "Oh say can you see? By da da da dumm dummm . . . ."

Unfortunately, it was a forgettable performance. But the fight itself has never been forgotten. At the opening bell, the heavyweights lunged out of their respective corners and began sizing one another up, a little poke here, a jab there. We all settled in for the promised slugfest. Then suddenly, two minutes and twenty seconds later, to be exact, the whole thing was over. Liston lay dazed on the canvas, with the young Ali taunting him to get up and fight. What? Was there a punch thrown? Did Liston take a dive? What the heck happened, anyway?

Bill Green tells me (He knows about this stuff. I made the mistake of betting against him one evening in a bar about thirty years ago and I've never done *that* again.) that the only person who actually *saw* the punch was Governor John H. Reed. According to the Gov, "That was a helluva punch Clay threw."

The rest, as they say, is history. The celebs left town. Goulet's voice and career survived the evening, and although folks might refer to him as "The Greatest!" *nobody* makes the mistake of calling Muhammad Ali Cassius Clay anymore.

## M AINE  S CHOOL  OF  S CIENCE  AND  M ATHEMATICS
### *L i m e s t o n e*

T he Maine School of Science and Mathematics was founded
because of a good idea: Bring together the top minds in
science and math from around the state and give them a
first-rate high school education. But the school also embodies a
not-so-good idea: Locate the school as far away as possible from
any of the state's population centers.

Limestone, Maine, is in northern Aroostook County, about
the same distance from Portland as Portland is from New York
City. The town was the site of Loring Air Force Base, an outpost
of the Cold War that became obsolete and closed up in the mid-
1990s, leaving a vacant military facility and a lot of space in
town. The legislature selected the town as the site for a
"magnet" school for math and science. Some kids were attracted
to the idea; others were repelled.

Today, there are about 190 students in attendance in three
grades at the school, according to Dottie Martin, the executive
director. They come from all sixteen counties, and all are
residents at the school. In 1995, the first year of the school's
existence, the kids lived in a barracks at Loring; now they have
a residence hall on campus. Some local folks serve as host
families, offering homelike experiences for young kids far away
from their own families.

Despite the amenities, it must be lonely and desolate. To
some youngsters it's the equivalent of going to Siberia, with
long winters and not a lot of people. But to a lot of kids, there's
an advantage to being in such a remote spot. Student Senate
President Tim Bates comes from the town of Sebago, a little
smaller in size than Limestone but a lot closer to the bright

lights of the big city of Portland. Tim says the isolation helps with concentrating on the work. "Academics is the big focus," he says. He sees the school as an "excellent opportunity" that he might not otherwise have had.

Dottie Martin says the key to preventing kids from going stir-crazy is to keep them active. There are a lot of skiing activities, both cross-country and downhill, and mandatory recreation times. There's a pool, there are movies and mall visits, and some students attend local churches. The sports teams play as part of the Limestone school teams because the magnet school isn't big enough to field its own teams.

Despite its location, the Maine School of Science and Mathematics is gaining in popularity. Director Dottie Martin says that the number of interested applicants increases each year, due in good measure to word of mouth recommendations from graduates who have now completed college. The opportunity is there for the right type of person to be drawn to magnetic north.

## THE SWEET WATERS OF BITHER BROOK
### Linneus

There aren't many Bithers in this world. A good proportion of them live in the state of Maine; of those, a good portion have roots or connections in Aroostook County. In the town of Linneus, there are a lot of Bithers. Unfortunately, most of them are in the town cemetery on the hill overlooking the fields and forests of this rural community.

All Bithers are related, in some way. There was one Bither (called Biter), who started the clan back in the 1700s. He lived in southern Maine. Some of his descendants moved to the wilderness of Aroostook County and set up homes and farms.

My grandfather, Milton J. Bither, was born in 1878, and he lived for a time in Linneus with his many brothers and sisters. One of the Bithers married a cousin, also named Bither (well, the Roosevelts did the same thing!), but that was not in my lineage. My father, Donald Bither, spent his first twelve years on the family farm in Linneus, taking care of the sheep and the horses, chores that he hated. He went to the one-room schoolhouse until he graduated from eighth grade. Then he went into the big town of Houlton to attend Ricker Classical Institute as a boarding student.

People's names often are used to describe places, like Washington County. Even the town of Linneus has a nominal heritage—it's named for the Swedish botanist, Carolus Linnaeus. But not every family has its own river.

My family does. It's called Bither Brook.

Bither Brook runs between the Meduxnekeag River in New Limerick and Sawyer Pond in Linneus. The brook, not more than 6 feet wide at its greatest width, runs through the same woods and fields that my grandfather and father tramped around in long ago. When we were boys on a visit to the county, we cut down a sapling branch, baited our hooks with local worms, and caught little trout lurking in the same shady pools that *their* great grandparents had hidden in.

A few years ago, my brothers took our father to visit the site of his old homestead, which had burned down and been abandoned many years ago. We made a stop at the spot where Bither Brook travels through a culvert under the road. My brothers and I took off our shoes and socks and dipped our toes in the cool water splashing over the rocks.

The Hindus make their pilgrimage to the Ganges; Western religions speak of crossing the Jordan. Here, in the backwoods of Aroostook County, is a shrine just as sacred, but only to those few people who carry the Bither name. To some people, it's just a little trickle of water. But to a Bither, the water in this brook flows in our veins, and washing our feet in it reminds us of who we are and where we came from.

# NEW HAMPSHIRE LIQUOR STORE ON THE CIRCLE

**T**here are several out-of-state locations where you will meet a lot of Mainers. Some trailer parks in Florida are dotted with cars from Maine snowbirds. The buses at Foxwoods casino in Connecticut carry more parishioners from Maine churches than show up at Sunday services. But one place you are guaranteed to encounter a substantial number of your fellow Maine residents is at a New Hampshire liquor store.

On a weekday in June, there were sixty-two cars in the parking lot of the Portsmouth liquor store, a number that presumably includes those belonging to the employees of the store. Nineteen of the vehicles had Maine plates. This number is easily enough to make a quorum for an AA meeting.

One can purchase liquor at a "discount" store in the state of Maine, if one is suitably equipped with a compass, global positioning equipment, and decent shock absorbers to protect against the potholes in the parking lot. The Kittery store is not easy to find, and its prices aren't always a terrific discount. This is because the government of Maine is ambivalent, at best, about selling booze, dating back to the days of the "green front" state stores, and perhaps back to Prohibition days. The government also takes some flak from people who complain that there is one price for folks in southern Maine and a much higher price for everyone else.

New Hampshire, on the other hand, has a pragmatic approach. It wants your money. It probably hopes you buy the booze and go drink it in another state. So New Hampshire has easy-to-locate stores, right off I–95. It has a big selection, good prices, and no sales taxes. And it has Mainers.

*Mainers stopping by the New Hampshire liquor store for a fresh fifty-five gallon drum of coffee brandy.*

How can you tell that there are Mainers in the New Hampshire store? They're the ones that ask for the coffee brandy, Maine's official beverage. They probably won't go to the single-malt Scotch section. And whatever they buy, it's in bulk. A common phrase in Portland is "I've got to go to New Hampshire soon." They put their big boxes of booze in the trunks of their cars and head home. Meanwhile, the clerks in Kittery dust off the bottles and look out the window at the empty potholed parking lot.

## THE MOXIE MAN
### Lisbon Falls

You've got moxie! That is, you *will* have Moxie by the time you leave the Moxie store in Lisbon Falls. At least, you will if the Moxie Man has anything to say about it, and believe me, he has plenty to say about it. The Moxie Man is Frank Annescetti, whose mission in life seems to involve proselytizing, evangelizing, and otherwise spreading the Gospel of Moxie to anyone who will lend an ear or an untutored palate.

What is Moxie? In its heyday, back in the 1920s and '30s, any schoolchild could have answered that question. Back then (according to Frank, a virtual encyclopedia of Moxie trivia, legend, and lore), Moxie was the most popular soft drink in the nation. Swilled and ballyhooed by sports legends like Ted Williams and an impressive roster of big-name Hollywood stars, Moxie led all other soft drinks in sales, with Coca-Cola trailing a distant second.

The original formula for the drink was concocted by a Maine man, and its name (Frank says it's most likely a variation of the name of a Maine Indian chief) added a new word to the American lexicon. According to the latest *American Heritage* Dictionary, *moxie* means "the ability to face difficulty with spirit and courage" also "aggressive energy and initiative." That second definition really hits home with me because as far as I'm concerned, just drinking the stuff takes a sizable dollop of "aggressive energy and initiative."

To put it bluntly, the stuff tastes awful. Oddly enough, the Moxie Man wouldn't necessarily disagree. He once described the experience of drinking Moxie this way: "You take your first sip, and it doesn't taste that good. Then you take another sip, and it still tastes kinda strong, bitter, like that. Then you take another sip . . . ." The way Frank describes initiation into the Moxie

*Never heard of Moxie?*
*Frank wants you!!!!*

Drinkers Club, you never actually get to *liking* the stuff. You more or less just *get used* to it.

But who cares what I think? To folks like Frank and the legions of Moxie fans who make the annual trek to Lisbon Falls for Moxie Day, the second Saturday in July (Moxie addicts from as far away as the British Isles gather for a sip of the sacred elixir), there's just nothing like the taste of Moxie. On that point we agree.

When pressed, Moxie drinkers often describe the taste as bitter. "It's not sweet," they point out, as if sweet soft drinks were solely responsible for the moral decline of Western democracies. Grasping for something the listener can identify with, they earnestly liken its pungent flavor to things like castor oil, horseradish, and bitter herb tea. Does that make you want to run right out and buy a six-pack? I didn't think so.

But buy it they do. The Moxie store has Moxie and Diet Moxie (I can only assume that it's even less sweet than the original Moxie, a terrifying thought) by the case and carton, as well as a massive array of T-shirts, sweatshirts, bumper stickers (MOXIE MAKES MAINERS MIGHTY!), Frisbees, key chains, and the like, all in the distinctive orange-and-black colors of the original logo. Maybe there should be a bumper sticker that reads IT'S ALWAYS HALLOWEEN WHEN YOU DRINK MOXIE!

Whatever else can be said about Moxie, it's clear that Moxie fans will go to great lengths to satisfy their exotic tastes. The Moxie Man is, of course, happy to help out. He does a brisk business filling orders from around the country and has shipped cases of the beverage to such distant locales as Taiwan and Moscow.

Sadly, though, even surrounded by a sea of Moxie, Frank Annescetti will never be completely satisfied. The Moxie Man finally, grudgingly, acknowledged that today's Moxie pales by comparison to the original. "I remember the original Moxie," he admits wistfully, "not this kid's stuff of today. Back then you would never open a bottle warm. You'd want the bottle ice cold. If not" (he snaps his fingers loudly, in a dramatic imitation of the sound of an old-time Moxie bottle cap popping off) "half of it's on your ceiling. The extra carbonation that was in it . . . the extra bitterness . . . ." His voice trails off into a sigh.

What? Today's Moxie isn't as bitter as the original . . . as potent? Opening a bottle won't knock out a streetlamp 3 blocks away? No offense, Frank, but some of us would consider that a sign of progress.

## WORUMBO MILL
### Lisbon Falls

The remaining buildings of the Worumbo Mill on the banks of the Androscoggin stand as a monument to a day when Lisbon Falls was the center of the universe, and to the lessons learned from a one-crop economy. Some of the buildings are from the late 1800s, and a major addition was made in 1920. Many of the buildings were lost in a fire in the early 1990s. But Worumbo still stands and is still operating.

In its heyday, in the first part of the twentieth century, the locally owned Worumbo Mill manufactured woolen products. Trainloads of fine wool from around the country would arrive at the mill, to be dyed, spun, and woven into woolen blankets and woolen fabrics for clothing. Children of nomadic tribes would gather camel hair, to be made into coats. Children of South American mountain villages would gather the hair of vicuña, which would be sent to Lisbon Falls, where it would be turned into an elegant, expensive, and trendy fabric. During the Eisenhower administration, a scandal erupted when it was discovered that a presidential adviser had accepted a gift of a vicuña coat. Fabrics made by the Worumbo Mill were recognized around the world for their high quality.

The mill was the biggest employer in the village of Lisbon Falls, where the houses clustered on nearby hillsides housed some French Canadians, some Yankees, and many Slovaks, who contributed to the culture of the town (ask about the Upper Slovak Club and the Lower Slovak Club). There was a turkey at Christmas; there was a summer picnic and a baseball team; and the wages were, arguably, enough to live on. But the textile industry was unstable. In the late 1950s the owners of the mill sold out to J. P. Stevens Company, which closed the mill in the1960s and moved its textile operations down south.

A series of owners, with assistance from the town, tried, with only minimal success, to keep the mill going. Finally, Herman Miller, who owned other textile mills in the area, acquired the mill and its machinery. It was then that Worumbo came into its own. This worldwide center of spinning fine fabrics from many lands became the home of, you guessed it, polyester. The same looms that once wove fine vicuña coats for the powerful and well-to-do now warped and woofed their way into powder blue leisure suits donned at gatherings of mere common folk.

In addition to the mixed blends, the hundred-year-old looms now spin and weave cotton-based fabric. According to Allan Miller, Herman's nephew, the wool process adds a special texture to the cotton. The mill makes a variety of fabrics and products, including blankets sold in stores around the country.

In the Worumbo Mill Outlet store, you will see, in addition to the fabrics and products, spools and cogs from the old looms and an account book from the early 1900s. You will also see, along the walls of the store, large photographs of the men, women, and children, proudly standing at their machines and asking, across the chasm of time, "What the hell is polyester?"

## ALL ROADS LEAD FROM ROME TO LYNCHVILLE
### Lynchville

I t's an icon of Maine kitsch, a picture of the sign that points the way to China, Paris, Norway, Peru, and other exotic lands, all, of course, located within the boundaries of our great state. The sign can have several meanings—one is that all the world's pleasures and needs are right outside our doorway. But do the towns have anything to do with their names? There isn't even a Chinese restaurant in China, although you can get an Italian sandwich in Rome and french fries in South Paris.

Most Mainers who know the sign may have a distant memory of seeing it as a child, when in fact it was really just the picture. Does this sign really exist? Or is it like the guys they supposedly put on the moon when they were really in the desert?

*"You can't get there from here?" Why not? The whole world's practically in our backyard.*

And if it does exist, how do you get there? I contacted John Stanley of the Maine Department of Transportation, and he had to look at the maps to find it. From Norway, you go to East Waterford, then head west to North Waterford, and you're almost there. Now, from West Paris, go to Bethel, then go south; where Routes 5 and 35 join together, keep on going. Of course, if you're coming from Sweden, you would take Route 5 north through Lovell, then head west toward East Stoneham. If you're coming from Berlin, which is in New Hampshire, you might as well be coming from Athens.

All of these roads meet up in the little village of Lynchville, where, at the convergence (or separation) of Routes 5 and 35, the world-weary sign stands. It's all well and good if you want to go to one of these places, but I still can't get to East Vassalboro. What's that, you say? It's right next to China? Ayuh, you could look it up.

# MIDNIGHT (OR NOON) AT THE OASIS AT IRVING MAINEWAY

They are everywhere along the highways of Maine, these oases for travelers. On a fog-shrouded night, the temple of Irving looms in the foreground, its structures and equipment bathed in welcoming light.

You might ask, what's so special about an Irving Maineway, a chain store that offers gas and sells cigarettes, coffee, and candy bars? A small number of Mainers will tell you what's so special.

You see, we are a frugal people; in fact, some folks might say we are cheap. We do not like to spend money on frivolities, and we do frequent places where our resources will be used wisely.

OK, but an Irving Maineway? The gas is the same price as elsewhere; the candy bars and beer are maybe higher than you would pay at a discount store. No, it's not that.

It's the hot dogs.

If you grumble about having to pay more than three bucks for a hamburger dinner at a place with arches, then you will feed yourself for less at Irving Maineway.

Near the back of the store, along one counter, slightly littered with empty ketchup containers and paper scraps, located next to the coffee creamers, and right above the trash container, you will find, side by side, two steam-type vessels, one containing packages with hot dog buns, and one with steamed, red-snapper hot dogs. Taking care not to burn or scald yourself, you simply pull out two rolls, take out two of the dogs (that have been sitting there for quite a while, so you know they've been cooked properly), slather them with condiments (leaving the condiment packages on the counter), get a napkin, go up to the counter, and pay . . . 99 cents.

That's right, Mr. Man, 99 cents for two dogs. Now, some fancier Irving Maineways have higher overhead costs, and you might have to pay $1.29 for two dogs. But it's still cheaper, and faster, than the arches. You fill yourself up until you reach home, or the next Irving Maineway. And your caravan heads off into the night, leaving the lights of the oasis glittering for the next cheap, hungry traveler.

# WE BREED 'EM, YOU FEED 'EM
## *Machias*

J ust like potholes, frost heaves, and ankle-deep mud, the
arrival of the blackfly is a sure sign of spring in the state
of Maine. Great clouds of the bloodthirsty critters cruise
fields, farms, forests, and front porches looking for fresh
victims. To fully appreciate the work of the Maine Blackfly
Breeders Association, based in Machias, you should know a little
bit about our local humor. The notion of discovering and
awakening the laughter that lies dormant in life's difficulties
(long winters, poor economy, death and taxes, etc.) is a central
recurring theme in Maine humor.

This "when life hands you lemons, make lemonade" attitude
is clearly the driving force behind the MBBA. How else are you
going to explain the hundreds of bumper stickers in parking
lots across the state proudly proclaiming SAVE THE BLACKFLY and
BLACKFLY BREEDERS ASSOCIATION: WE BREED 'EM, YOU FEED 'EM! or
the brisk sales of items like handmade miniature blackfly
houses not much bigger than a postage stamp.

According to Holly Garner-Jackson, Marilyn Dowling, and
Jim Wells, the current keepers of the MBBA flame, the whole
thing began a few years back when writer Peter Crolius penned
a series of tongue-in-cheek articles in support of the blackfly for
local newspapers. In the aftermath of the writer's death a few
years later, talented local sign painter and illustrator Marilyn
Dowling promised the author's daughter that she and her
friends would carry on the important work Peter had started.

And carry it on they did, in fine style. The MBBA won first
prize in the Machias Fourth of July parade. As their float (a
giant blackfly, of course) rolled by, volunteers ran into the
crowd placing red stickers on bystanders' faces indicating that
they'd been "bitten." Shortly thereafter, the MBBA sought and

received official nonprofit status so that the loot from their big Fourth of July win ($1,000), along with proceeds from the sale of their growing line of blackfly products (my personal favorite being the snowstorm-style glass paperweight, which when shaken stirs up a cloud of tiny blackflies), would benefit local charities.

Where does the MBBA go from here? The sky (what you can see of it through the clouds of blackflies, that is) is the limit. You might want to check out their Web site, www.maineblackflybreeders.com for details. Good luck, and as we say up here in Maine, "May the swarm be with you."

## JAMIE WYETH: ARTIST IN A BOX
### Monhegan Island

Monhegan Island may well be the closest thing there is to a physical manifestation of the artist's muse. Generations of painters and photographers have made the pilgrimage to Monhegan and criss-crossed its granite and spruce contours seeking creative inspiration. The list of famous painters who have sought to capture the island's beauty includes such luminaries of American art as Rockwell Kent and Winslow Homer.

Of course, any list of famous American artists would be incomplete without Jamie Wyeth. Son of Andrew Wyeth and grandson of legendary illustrator N. C. Wyeth, Jamie is a brilliant painter in his own right. During a recent interview on the deck of his Monhegan home, Wyeth mentioned that he was only sixteen years old when he purchased the house from Rockwell Kent. When I exhibited my usual lack of tact and refinement by asking him where a sixteen-year-old would get that kind of cash, he said simply, "I sold a few of my paintings."

So the guy can paint, OK? But painting is a solitary endeavor, almost a form of meditation. So how, on an island crawling with tourists (not to mention other painters), does a man as famous as Wyeth manage to work with any degree of privacy? "Well," he said, "I paint in a box." Yup, you heard right, and according to Jamie Wyeth, it's a very effective tool. He stays out of the wind and weather, and most folks aren't quite snoopy enough to come up and peek in.

So, maybe I let the cat out of the bag (or the artist out of the box?) here, but, please, PLEASE, do me and Mr. Wyeth a favor. If you happen to find yourself traipsing around Monhegan Island someday and you notice a man making a painting in a box, DO NOT go over and bother the guy. Maybe you can just take a snapshot of the box or something. But let it go at that, alright? If ever there was an appropriate spot to paste one of those QUIET: GENIUS AT WORK! stickers, this would be it. Just let the man paint. Whatever masterpiece he's working on is likely to show up at a museum near you eventually, and when folks ask you if you've seen it yet, you can just flash 'em a mysterious Mona Lisa smile and say, "No. But I *have* seen the box it came in."

## *ZOE ZANIDAKIS, LOBSTERWOMAN?*
### *Monhegan Island*

I first met Zoe Zanidakis when she was hired by CBS News to ferry my producer, my camera crew, and me back to the mainland after a day spent on Monhegan Island discussing the history of painting on the island with Jamie Wyeth. It was clear from the moment we set foot on her awesomely shipshape 40-foot Young Brothers lobster boat, the *Equinox,* that, despite her gender and relative youth (mid-thirties), Zoe was

*Call her a "pin-up girl" if you want. But don't say I never warned you.*

unquestionably the captain of the vessel. We cast off and headed back to Boothbay Harbor, and over the thrum and roar of the powerful diesel engine I made the mistake of asking her if she was originally from "around here."

The look she gave me was akin to the one Captain Ahab must have given Moby Dick just before he tossed the harpoon, and she informed me that she was, in fact, a "seventh-generation Monhegan Island fisherman." Smackdown on the high seas! I couldn't have felt more idiotic if I'd asked Wyeth the younger whether any other members of his family had ever dabbled at art. Since it's a long swim back to the mainland, I felt fortunate that years of toting city slickers around the wild North Atlantic have inured Zoe to bonehead remarks like mine. Otherwise, I'd probably be writing this from Davy Jones's locker.

Zoe first ventured onto the rolling deck of a lobster boat (her grandfather's) at the tender age of six months. The rest, as they say, is history—seven generations of it, no less. By the time she was in high school she'd already been working on the water for several years. She landed her first full-time job as a sternman while still in her teens and had her own boat, a 36-footer, at age twenty-two. She's been fishing ever since.

Like other Monhegan lobstermen, Zoe fishes "the season," from Trap Day on December 1 to Haul Out on May 29. When I asked her how many traps she tends, I felt stupid all over again. "The limit's 600," she said matter-of-factly, as if only an idiot would consider hauling even one trap fewer than the maximum allowed by law. In the off months Zoe makes a living as a certified scuba diver, running charter fishing trips or ferrying passengers to various destinations along the coast.

But lest you think that this bright, attractive, seafaring lady is all work and no play, she assures me that her credo has always been "If you work hard, you gotta play hard." When we spoke the other day, she was doing a bit of playing, autographing her photo in the 2002 edition of the "Lobster Women of Maine" calendar. That's right, Cap'n Zoe (born on St. Patrick's Day) is Miss March. But don't get the wrong idea. She's fully clothed, standing confidently at the helm of the *Equinox,* looking every inch the hardworking lobsterwoman she is.

Lobsterwoman? Lobsterlady? Lobsterperson? Just what does one call a female lobsterman, anyway? "I'm a Monhegan Island lobsterman," she replies simply, obviously disdainful of lesser monikers, adding by way of explanation, "Go down to the island post office and ask the lady behind the counter how she likes being referred to as a 'postmistress.'" I politely declined Zoe's kind offer on the grounds that I'd already asked enough foolish questions for one day.

## A NEW LIFE FOR CUMSTON HALL
### Monmouth

Town halls in Maine are located in a variety of building types. Some are in trailers or modular buildings, some in abandoned schoolhouses, some in nondescript, functional brick-and-mortar buildings that have no character, and some in buildings that bespeak the importance of the governmental process going on within. But there is one former town hall that is a crown jewel of architecture. That is Cumston Hall, in the center of the small (population 3,350) town of Monmouth.

Cumston Hall, built in 1900, is a mix of architectural styles, from Romanesque towers and columns to Queen Anne–style textures. It seems too ornate, and yet too delicate, to serve as a public building. When it was constructed, it was ahead of its time because it boasted of indoor plumbing and electricity. It is listed on the National Register of Historic Buildings.

Cumston Hall is no longer the site for Monmouth's town hall. In the late 1990s, the town moved its operations to a more functional structure down the road. However, Cumston Hall still houses the town library.

In addition, ten thousand people visit Cumston Hall each summer to attend performances at the Theater at Monmouth, a professional theater company that performs Shakespearean fare in the hall's 250-seat theater, originally styled as an opera house. For several years in the 1950s, the theater was home to a Gilbert and Sullivan company. Gilbert and Sullivan operettas are still staged during the off-season. For more information on performances of the Theater at Monmouth, call (207) 933–9999.

*Cumston Hall. Not your ordinary New England town hall.*

# MANY BRIDGES TO CROSS

**O**K, so you have the outline of every state on the side of your Winnebago, meaning you've been there and done that in the lower forty-eight. And maybe you can boast, unlike most Mainers, that you have spent a night in each of Maine's sixteen counties. But here's a checklist for the day traveler, one that combines history, geography, and two centuries of bridge-building technology. The Maine Department of Transportation has compiled a list of bridges (not including pedestrian and railroad bridges) that cross the Kennebec River, from the Atlantic Ocean to Moosehead Lake. How many of these have you crossed? Can you identify the persons or places for whom the bridges are named? Here they are:

| LOCATION | NAME |
|---|---|
| Bath–Woolwich | Carlton (old and newly reconstructed as Sagadahoc) |
| Richmond–Dresden | Maine Kennebec |
| Gardiner–Randolph | Gardiner Randolph (who was that guy, Gardiner Randolph, anyway?) |
| Augusta | Memorial (in memory of whom? I forget) |
| Augusta | Father John J. Curran |
| Waterville–Winslow | Donald V. Carter |
| Waterville–Winslow | Ticonic |
| Fairfield | Kennebec River East-Center-West |
| Fairfield | Clinton A. Clausen Bridges |
| Hinckley | George W. Hinckley |
| Skowhegan | Margaret Chase Smith Bridges |
| Norridgewock | Covered |
| Madison–Anson | Bicentennial Memorial |
| Embden–Solon | Embden-Solon (not the most original name for a bridge) |
| Bingham–Concord | Kennebec River |
| The Forks | The Forks |
| Sapling Township | East Outlet Bridge |
| Taunton–Raynham Academy Grant | West Outlet Bridge (I thought all of the outlets were in Freeport) |

As we mentioned, this list does not include railroad bridges—these have their own history and charm—and pedestrian bridges. An example of the latter is the bridge between Winslow and Waterville used by thousands of mill workers who either couldn't afford or didn't need an automobile to get them where they had to go.

## THE MONSON RAILROAD: THE WORLD'S WORST LITTLE RAIL LINE
### *Monson*

The Monson Railroad is one of the least illustrious rail lines in Maine transportation history. According to town history, the railroad was created in the 1880s because the Grand Trunk Railroad was laying out its tracks on a route that would bypass the town of Monson.

Perhaps to right an insult, or thinking that there might be a niche to fill, an entrepreneur set up a 6-mile, narrow-gauge road from Monson to Monson Junction. An additional 2 miles connected the road with the slate quarries. The little locomotive, called the "Peanut Roaster," never turned around. It just went forward 6 miles one way and backwards the other. The train, designed primarily to haul slate, also carried some passengers and some mail and freight. But not very well, and never at a profit. There's also the following poem, written by one H.D.

*The Monson Railroad used to run*
*Three or four trains a day for fun.*
*But their net profits the whole year through*
*Wouldn't buy the engineer one drink of home brew.*
*So after twenty years they changed their style*
*And now they only run a train once in a while.*
*Their timetable hangs there high on the wall*
*And looks like a blank sheet with a pencil scrawl.*
*Come over quite close or there's something you'll miss*
*And you'll find that the timetable reads something like this:*
*Train number one on track number two*
*Leaves Monson whenever they can find their crew,*
*If the weather is fair and the wind doesn't blow*
*They'll be back with the mail in a day or so.*

Mercifully for all, the Monson Railroad folded in 1945.

*Ayuh. Here in Maine, one man's junk is another man's coffee table.*

*There's bound to be something useful in there. Just keep lookin'.*

## THE UMBRELLA COVER MUSEUM
### Peaks Island

**M**any objects of everyday life have stories to tell. Just bring your imagination to any yard sale and you will find items with history—the chest of drawers with the bullet hole, the teapot with the chipped spout, the dog-eared paperback with illegible margin notes—if they could talk, we would hear a story. Maybe not an interesting story, but it would be a story.

And so it is with umbrella covers—the tube-like sleeves, sometimes called "sheaths" or "pockets," that keep umbrellas neat and tidy. According to Nancy 3. Hoffman, the proprietress of the Umbrella Cover Museum on Peaks Island, "Each cover has a story behind it." The Umbrella Cover Museum is dedicated to "the appreciation of the mundane in everyday life," says Hoffman, who runs the museum out of her home (visits by appointment only; 207–766–4496). Appreciation of umbrella covers is part of the appreciation of the wonder and beauty in the simplest of things.

Hoffman started collecting umbrella covers about six years

*Nancy 3. Hoffman.*
*Yep, that's her middle name.*

*The Umbrella Cover Museum boasts covers from around the world.*
*Here's an interesting place to spend a rainy day.*

ago, when some friends of hers couldn't bear to throw them out, "because they were too cute." A critical mass of covers developed, and now the museum boasts more than 300, including several new handmade covers, particularly admired for their symmetry.

The sheaths range in color and style from basic black to multi-patterned, and in materials from nylon to bullet-proof Kevlar. Hoffman bemoans the fact that umbrella manufacturers today either don't include or encase their products in clear plastic. "They've eliminated one of the last relics of tangible evidence of our civilized society," she says.

When she's not curating the mundane, Nancy 3. Hoffman plays accordion with the Maine Squeeze and with the Casco Bay Tummlers.

## P.U. IN PERU

*Peru*

t's not a roadside oddity, so much as a roadway occurrence. It's a combination of geography, the prevailing winds, and the nature of business and industry in the state of Maine.

When you're driving north on Route 108 from Auburn toward Rumford, you'll notice it, at first subtly, then unmistakably. In a car full of guys, someone might say, "Who cut the cheese?" In a family vehicle, the mother might inquire, "Has someone been indiscreet?" But everyone will notice it. It's the rotten egg, boiled cabbage smell of the paper mill in nearby Rumford as it wafts its way eastward and down the Androscoggin Valley. The mill makes kraft paper, using a type of high-sulfur process that produces the odor. Some local people call it "the sweet smell of success"; others claim it is a warning of the presence of dangerous chemicals.

When we were kids, the first time we'd notice it was in the town of Peru, about 15 miles downriver but before you got to town. When we were kids, we used to say "P.U." when something smelled bad (I'm not sure what that stood for). So, even today, when I go through Peru—despite the Incan heritage, or the nice farms and houses—all I can think of is this: "Here we are in Peru. Peeeeeee yewwwwwww."

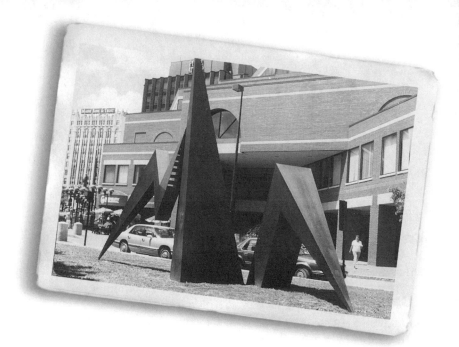

Take your pick—
modern or traditional?
Newfangled and classic
images of Maine are
situated just a few
yards apart in
downtown Portland.
The modern sculpture
at top is named Michael.
Michael who? As for the
Maine Lobsterman
statue below, nobody
even knows this guy's
name.

## THE TINFOIL MAN: IT'S NOT JUST FOR WRAPPING LEFTOVERS ANYMORE
### *Portland*

**H**is name is Robert Wilson, but just about everybody knows him simply as the Tinfoil Man. Robert's a warm, personable fellow with a soft southern drawl. His unique and fanciful sculptures are painstakingly handcrafted from tinfoil. It's the same shiny metallic wrap you have on your kitchen shelf; by the time he's done with a roll, though, you wouldn't recognize the stuff. His creations may be found lurking behind counters and peeking out of display windows in some of the trendiest shops in Portland's fashionable Old Port district.

*The street is always crowded when the "Tinfoil Man" does his thing.*

*Just one more in a loooong line of tinfoil scorpions.*

It's clear that Robert hasn't had the easiest life, but he never complains. Born in Alabama in 1956, he describes himself as a child without playmates. He started amusing himself by making fanciful animal pals out of scraps of discarded tinfoil when he was only six years old. He says his first creation was a scorpion (still one of his most popular designs) inspired by a classic '50s B-horror flick called *The Black Scorpion*.

Life has handed Robert more than a few rough breaks, but through it all he has continued to perfect and refine his tinfoil-sculpting technique. He eventually landed in a Portland homeless shelter over a decade ago. The shelter's manager, a woman he refers to only as Rita, took an interest in his work and suggested that he try and sell some of it. He took her up on it and was soon selling tiny, amazingly detailed tinfoil replicas of scorpions, parrots, and dragonflies. Although his prices were modest—24 cents each at first—the entrepreneurial spark was obviously there as well. "I knew they'd tell me to just keep the quarter," he explains with a grin.

The Tinfoil Man estimates that, with roughly an hour of his life invested in each piece, he has created over 10,000 sculptures over the past forty years or so. Mostly they are animals: elephants, deer, moose, parrots, and his trademark scorpions, of course, with an occasional tyrannosaurus rex tossed in for variety. Every now and then he'll accept a commission. That's how he came to make the elaborate, lifelike Elvis sculpture that sits behind the counter of a hip upscale downtown Portland shoe store. It's The King, alright, complete with silver suede shoes and a really tinny looking guitar.

As so often happens in the art world, as the popularity of Robert's work increased, so did his fees. The Tinfoil Man now charges between $10 and $25 for a piece of tinfoil sculpture, and he's getting plenty of work. He's long since moved out of the homeless shelter and has a comfortable studio space. But he still likes to set up his wares on a sunny street corner and amaze pedestrians with what amounts to a form of performance art. Occasionally he'll meet up with somebody he knew back at the shelter. "The shock is sometimes a bit much," says Robert. "They look at me like I just fell out of a flying saucer."

As well they might. Clearly the Tinfoil Man is on his way up. He speaks enthusiastically of starting his own company and broadening his market share. He's even got the name picked out: With It Productions. I, for one, wouldn't bet against this guy. Robert Wilson is, pardon the pun, a "shining example" of what can happen when raw talent, hard work, and a bit of encouragement at a key moment combine to make a dream come true.

# ITALIAN SANDWICHES ARE THE REAL MAINE FOOD

If you went into a store in the North End of Boston, or in Providence, Rhode Island, and said, "Gimme a couple of Italians, and easy on the oil," you probably would not survive the encounter. But in Maine, as in nowhere else in the world (including Italy), a request for an "Eyetalian" will get you an oversize hot dog–type roll, stuffed with ham or salami, American or provolone cheese, tomatoes, onions, pickles, green peppers, and black olives, liberally drenched with olive oil, and sprinkled with salt and "peppa." For less than three bucks, you can get a quick, cheap, filling meal that isn't too bad for you.

Italian sandwiches are the bread and butter of hundreds of mom-and-pop stores. Everyone has a favorite place, including the one that claims to have invented them, Amato's on India Street in Portland. My father used to walk a mile from his downtown Portland office to Mrs. DiBiase's store at the foot of Munjoy Hill to get her version, which was loaded with Greek olives. No real Mainer would be caught ordering whatever they serve up at a Subway store.

A few years back, the same type of advertising genius who came up with "the new Coke" and "new and improved Tide" came up with the idea of a new name for an upgrade—either "Real Italian" or "Italian-style," which defines an Italian sandwich, only more so. One of these items may have more Genoa salami and provolone cheese; but otherwise, it's pretty much the same, except it costs more. The upgraded Italian-style and Real Italian sandwiches have their place, but they raise this question: What were we eating before we had "real" Italians?

When people "from away" think of food from Maine, they almost always think of "lobsta." But it's a safe assumption to say that Mainers consume more Italians per day, day in and day out, than they do lobsters. An Italian, whether it's called "real" or not, is real Maine food. Maybe we should put one on our license plate.

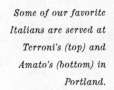

*Some of our favorite Italians are served at Terroni's (top) and Amato's (bottom) in Portland.*

### SITE OF LONGFELLOW'S SITE
#### Portland

Portland has markers or plaques that commemorate the first official hanging in the United States, that mark the spot of a brutal battle, and that honor a guy who used to walk up and down Congress Street and be friendly to everybody. Over on Fore Street, just south of the Eastern Promenade, there is a little indentation in the chain-link fence, and in that indentation is a rock. For many years, there was a plaque on the rock indicating that this was the site of the house where Portland's beloved bard, Henry ("Don't call me Hank") Longfellow was born. Then the plaque went missing, so there was just a rock. Now the plaque is baque.

The site of the birthplace begs the question: What is one supposed to do with such information? We're not talking about a manger, after all. The Longfellow House on Congress Street is open to the public. And, although Portlanders don't like to admit it, Longfellow wasn't really a superstar until he lived in Cambridge, Massachusetts.

The actual house where Longfellow was born was in existence until after World War II. It's mentioned in the *WPA Guide to Portland,* published in the late 1930s. Maybe a visitor could glean some knowledge, in those days, by viewing Henry's baby shoes or finding out what they did for diapers in the early 1800s. Or maybe there was some corner of the humble house where one could find the "lost youth" that Henry talked about:

> *There are things of which I may not speak;*
> *There are dreams that cannot die;*
> *There are thoughts that make the strong heart weak;*
> *And bring a pallor into the cheek,*
> *And a mist before the eye.*

*And the words of that fatal song*
*Come over me like a chill:*
*"A boy's will is the wind's will,*
*And the thoughts of youth are long, long thoughts."*

Now there's just a rock with a metal plate, marking the site where the long, long thoughts were carried away on the wind.

## *T IME AND T EMPERATURE*
### *Portland*

The old clock tower in many a village center is a welcome sign. It serves as a landmark. It stands as an indication of the importance of commerce in our everyday lives. The classic lines of clock faces speak of tradition—they are, in a sense, timeless.

But the forces of modernization are constantly at work, acting as if change is always better than tradition. Leisure suits come to mind as a modern improvement over the traditional vested men's suit. And so, the modern forces came to the time-telling function of the central city. Whether an improvement occurred is another matter.

The telephone company (back when there was just one telephone company) used to operate a digital-type time and temperature sign atop one of Portland's "skyscrapers" on Congress Street. Telling time digitally was all the rage. The sign was visible from many parts of the city, even in parts of the harbor. The sign wasn't as pretty as a clock, but it was there and it served its function.

When the phone company left, Maine Savings Bank moved in and added some words to the time and temperature sign, namely THE and BANK, which were flashed for several years.

Some people going through Portland would look up several times just to see an indefinite article flashing on a sign. "What's with THE anyway?" The bank folded in the late 1980s, and the sign went dark.

The building's owner, who was not locally connected, wanted simply to get rid of the sign. Starting it back up for operations would have violated the state's billboard law. Suddenly, the new, improved, modern time teller became a cause for preservationists. According to local attorney Lee Urban, the sign was "an icon." Lee encouraged local fund-raisers to kick in enough funds to get it started. The Chamber of Commerce managed the site, found advertisers, and added community messages (like SNOW BAN, to warn about parking during a snowstorm, and PLAY BALL, for the first day of Sea Dogs baseball). Lee convinced the legislature to amend the state's billboard law to get the sign flashing again. It took money to run. The lightbulbs, which look like pin dots from the street, are actually globes. Lee recalls going up to the sign on the top of the building and being concerned because the bulbs kept popping, which was expensive at $2.90 per bulb.

Today, the building is owned by the Libra Foundation, which was established by the wealthy philanthropist, Betty Noyce. This organization has fixed up the sign. The building on which the sign flashes once housed a magnificent movie and vaudeville theater. It once had an indoor mall, called the Arcade, with shops and restaurants for the very urbane. Important people, lawyers and business types, had their offices in the Civic Arcade Building. But now the tail wags the dog. Everyone who does business in the building, when giving directions to the office, says, "We're in the Time and Temperature Building."

## THE STUPIDEST PIECE OF PUBLIC ART
### *Portland*

"**I** don't know nothin' about art," the geezer told me. "But I do know what it ain't, and it ain't that." He was referring to three unidentifiable shapes of fabric sitting on poles in the water in Back Cove, Portland, just off the walking/running path that goes around the cove, parallel to Baxter Boulevard.

"Art is s'posed to imitate nature. Or else it should improve upon it," he continued. And in his mind, and to those of most passersby, this did neither. It just filled up a space and obstructed what would have been a nice view of the water.

*Put your underwear on a stick and set it in the harbor—that's art?*

"If I put my wife's underwear on some sticks and put 'em up at a scenic turnout on Route 1, they'd arrest me, and my wife would be some embarrassed." He was referring to the fact that one of the shapes looked like half a brassiere, and the others could also be some unmentionables. Or they could be luffed sails, I suggested. "Or they could be some other stupid thing," he continued. "But you ain't gonna tell me that they are art."

As for improving upon nature, the geezer pointed out, "Look over there at that sign [an interpretive sign near the road] describin' the wonders of nature to be found in the tidal waters of the cove. And remember, it was one of them tree-huggin' Baxters [James Phinney] who built the boulevard in hopes of preservin' nature." But this manmade art sits in the precious, teeming wetland, and it could disturb or alter nature's course.

"What I don't understand," the geezer continued, "is how the gov'ment—which has so many reg-a-lations about how close to the water you can put your camp and what kinda toilet you hafta have, and what you can put in your toilet—how that same gov'ment lets some lunkhead put up crap like that in the middle of the water, and all in the name of art."

Whereupon he shook his head again and said, "I just don't understand it." And he walked down the path to enjoy the rest of the view of the bay.

## SARDINE MAN WELCOMES YOU TO SARDINELAND
### Prospect Harbor

Sardine Man is distinguished from other Maine icons in several respects. First, he may be the only Maine giant to star in comic books (although Paul Bunyan might have snuck into a few). Second, he's the only big guy to start off in one location and end up in a new one just to avoid going to the dump.

*Maine's Sardine Ambassador. The big man with the big can full of little fish.*

Sardine Man is a 22-foot-tall, two-dimensional metal sculpture. He wears a yellow fisherman's outfit, including a rain hat, and carries the biggest can of sardines you'll ever see.

He originally stood at the entrance to the Maine Turnpike, according to Charlie Stinson, the former owner of Stinson Canning Company. He was owned by the Maine Sardine Council. "The council had a lot of collective marketing activities, including setting up one brand of sardines that all of the packers sold," Charlie says. Part of their marketing activities included postcards and comic books featuring youngsters in Sardineland.

As times changed, so did the public taste, and by the early 1980s, the council thought Sardine Man had outlived his usefulness. Ever the Yankee, Charlie Stinson heard they were going to take Sardine Man to the dump. "I told 'em, if you pay to take it down, I'll go get my wrecker and take it away," he says. "I wasn't going to pay to take it down if they were going to do it anyway." So, off went Sardine Man to his present site at the entrance of Stinson Seafood in Prospect Harbor. The original man had two decorated sides, "but I set it up so it only needed painting on one side," Charlie recalls. He had the man repainted once in the ensuing years.

The factory workers loved having Sardine Man there. The sardine workers in the old days had a lot to be proud of besides having Sardine Man out front. Getting sardines to the public involved a lot of effort. In the past, the fish were caught using stationary weirs, "when the fish come to you," says Charlie, instead of the purse-seining method used today, which has resulted in better catches, but in overfishing. "We used to dry some of the fish outdoors in the sun," he says, instead of the more automated system used today.

One thing that hasn't changed is the hand packing. "You get good workers with the little fish, about eight or ten to a can, and they can make some money," according to Charlie. In its promotional material, the Stinson Seafood Company boasts: "Regardless of size or product, every single can is packed by hand—over 65 million cans a year! No machine has ever been invented that could match the speed, skill, and care of our Maine packers."

The smaller herring have been overfished nowadays. The packers concentrate on cut-up fish steaks, and the company imports some herring from other parts of the world for processing and repacking. Automated equipment does the nonpacking work at the Prospect Harbor plant.

Charlie Stinson sold his sardine business in 1992, and the company, now called Stinson Seafood Company, has changed hands several times. Recently, the company downsized its operations substantially. When I called the Portland office for information about the Sardine Man, the person in charge said he didn't know anything about the sign because he'd never been to Prospect Harbor.

If he did bother to go to Prospect Harbor, though, he'd find an industry that dates to the late 1800s, a plant that was started by Carl Stinson (Charlie's father) in the 1920s, and a 22-foot guy holding the world's biggest can of sardines welcoming him to Sardineland.

## THE WILHELM REICH MUSEUM: "THE HOUSE THAT ORGASMS BUILT"
### *Rangeley*

Wilhelm Reich was either a "renowned physician/scientist" (according to the home page of the Wilhelm Reich Museum) or someone whose ideas had "no status in the scientific community" (according to *The Skeptics Dictionary* by Robert Todd Carroll; SkepDic.com).

Reich, an Austrian psychologist who lived from 1897 to 1957, conducted many of his experiments in Rangeley, Maine. He believed that there was a form of energy that could be detected, measured, and harnessed. To capitalize on this energy, which he termed "Orgone" in 1942, Reich created and sold orgone "accumulators" and orgone "shooters." These devices were banned in the 1950s by the Food and Drug Administration, which also burned some of Reich's books. Today, the Wilhelm Reich Museum in Rangeley features equipment used in his pioneering experiments as well as Reich's library, personal memorabilia, sculpture, and paintings.

What is this orgone stuff, anyway? It has something to do with orgasms. The "renowned scientist" described it as: "The ability for total surrender to the involuntary contractions of the orgasm and the complete discharge of the excitation at the acme of the genital embrace," which creates an "orgastic potency." In many places, such talk would get the authorities steamed up. But in Rangeley, most people probably couldn't figure out what he meant.

Those who disagreed with Reich, and there were many, were called "orgastically impotent." So it was just as well that folks in the area focused on Reich's rooftop observatory, which provides a spectacular view of the surrounding area.

Reich attempted to demonstrate his "orgonoscope" to Albert Einstein, in Princeton, New Jersey, but when was the last time someone from New Jersey listened to someone from Maine? One critic said that claimed results of the orgonoscope were suspect because Rangeley is so far north as to be affected by the aurora borealis, which in turn subjects the area to "high doses of cosmic rays." Maybe the presence of northern cosmic rays also explains why moose stand in the middle of the road at night.

Wilhelm Reich became a martyr to his ideas. He died in 1957, in Lewisburg Federal Penitentiary, where he was imprisoned for defying the FDA's ban on his products. His tomb, with its dramatic bronze bust, stands in a forest clearing near the museum. Some of Reich's ideas have not been fully released to the public, such as the "orgone-powered motor," which purportedly ran smoothly. This information is expected to be released sometime in this decade—just in time for the next energy crisis. Meantime, visitors to the museum can see the grounds, the guest cabins, and the scientific gizmos that go along with "the house that orgasms built."

# TOP TEN STUPID QUESTIONS
# (AND TEN SNAPPY ANSWERS)

**W**hile we do enjoy and appreciate the many tourists who come to Maine, people "from away" have been known to ask some pretty foolish questions. Here are a few of our favorites, along with some snappy responses.

Q. Do the lobstermen always park their boats in the same direction?

A. *Sure, and every few hours they come back and park them in the other direction.*

Q. Does each lobsterman tend his own traps?

A. *Nope. The traps are all owned by "summer people." The lobstermen just go out and haul 'em as a public service.*

Q. Can a person get a better price on lobster by dealing with the fisherman directly?

A. *Absolutely! Why don't you go down to the co-op this afternoon and ask for the manager? He'll tell you how it works.*

Q. (looking at live lobsters in a holding tank) Are they fresh?

A. *Yes, they tend to whistle and make crude comments whenever a pretty girl walks by.*

Q. Does this road go to Bangor?

A. *Nope. It stays right here.*

Q. How do you get to Portland from here?

A. *Generally, my brother-in-law takes me.*

Q. (from a tourist obviously loaded down with purchases made on vacation) Can we take this road all the way back to New York?

A. *You might as well. Looks like you've already taken about everything else.*

Q. Do you people always talk in that quaint dialect?

A. *Nope. After Labor Day we all switch to British accents.*

Q. Is it cold here in the winter?

A. *Of course not. People come here from Florida every January to get a tan.*

Q. You've been sitting on that porch for a long time. Don't you people work?

A. *Nope. Why do you think we call it Vacationland?*

## THE WGME TALL TOWER
### Raymond

**M**aine is home to a lot of big things—the Big Indians in Freeport and Skowhegan, the big Paul Bunyan in Bangor, the Big Cheese in Augusta. For a brief period of time, Maine was home to the tallest man-made structure in the world. This was during Maine's brief era of self-esteem, somewhere between the election of Clinton Clausen as governor and the Clay–Liston fight in Lewiston. Things were big. And so in 1959, the folks at the Guy Gannet Broadcasting Company built a television tower in Raymond that was 1,619 feet tall—taller than the Empire State Building, which was then recognized as the tallest building in the forty-eight states at 1,472 feet tall.

The tower was a monumental effort. Of course, its soaring height was surpassed in about six months by another TV tower somewhere. But it's still taller than the Empire State Building.

Today the engineers at the tower get to go up and down the elevator to the top, but they don't have to change the lightbulbs on the outside. Craig Clark, the chief engineer, says the tower may have been hit by lightning several times, but, thankfully, it's grounded. Some skydivers jumped off the platform a few years ago. Apparently, their chutes worked. Viewers of channel 13 news see the view taken from the camera on top of the tower, including storm patterns moving in over the lakes.

The tower will undergo some upgrading and renovation in the next couple of years. But it will still be bigger—by far—than the Empire State Building. It also happens to be taller than the Eiffel Tower (a mere 984 feet) and the Washington Monument (just 555 feet). Not that we Mainers like to brag or anything.

## THINK YOU'VE SEEN "THE LAST SHAKER"?
### THINK AGAIN
#### Sabbathday Lake

If you were among the millions of PBS viewers who tuned in to the Ken Burns documentary *The Last Shaker* a few years back, you can be excused for thinking that the Shakers, a small religious order who have made a big contribution to our modern American way of life, are an extinct breed. I'm pleased to report that nothing could be further from the truth. Far from being the spiritual equivalent of the passenger pigeon, you will find a half-dozen of these delightful folks alive and well and living in the Shaker community at Sabbathday Lake, in New Gloucester.

Here are a few things I learned while visiting the Shakers. First off, I had somehow formed the impression that Shakers were part of the austere, cranky, antitechnology religious crowd, sort of like the Amish in Pennsylvania. You know, dressing in black, driving buggies instead of cars, writing with charcoal on the back of shovels by candlelight, and so forth. No way!

The Shakers are, like, *way* into technology. As a matter of fact, they've been pretty much on the cutting edge of it since they first came to these shores from Manchester, England, back in 1774 and founded the Sabbathday Lake Community in 1783. In addition to designing and manufacturing the famous Shaker chairs and other furniture, the Shakers invented a lot of other cool stuff we use every day. The flat broom (as opposed to the round one the Wicked Witch of the West rode), the automatic washing machine, and even the dump truck are among the many inventions and innovations thought up by these pious, gentle, ingenious folks. By the way, in case you're thinking this

*The last Shaker? Not likely, bub! The*
*Shakers are alive and well in Maine.*

is some kind of "get rich with God" type of religion, forget it:
Shakers never bother to patent anything. When they build a
better mousetrap, they just give it to the world, their way of
saying, "Hey, God loves you!" Like I say, these are seriously
nice folks.

Shakers also have a long-standing tradition of offering a
free hot meal to any passing stranger in need of one. This has
led to some interesting encounters. Back at the turn of the
twentieth century, just such a vagrant, apparently an itinerant
tramp, stopped by, enjoyed a bit of Shaker hospitality, and went
on his way, fortified in body and spirit. It wasn't until a few
weeks later, when a package containing a handwritten thank-
you note and an expensive set of silver dinnerware arrived, that
the stranger's identity was revealed. The anonymous "tramp"
who came for dinner was none other than Louis Comfort
Tiffany.

They also just love to belt out a tune. Shaker hymns are for the most part lively and upbeat, not unlike the folks who sing them. Their big hit "Simple Gifts," written by Elder Joseph Brackett right at the Sabbathday Lake Community, speaks volumes about their way of life. You know, it's the song that begins, " 'Tis a gift to be simple. . . ." Since Shakers take a pledge of celibacy, they must rely on converts to keep the community going. Fortunately, there are currently two new novitiates living with the community. I, for one, hope these newcomers decide to take the pledge and join up when the time comes. The way I see it, the world is a lot better place with a few Shakers in it. Let's all hope the last Shaker is many, many lifetimes away.

## BILL O'NEILL'S "HOUSE OF ROCK 'N' ROLL"
### *Saco*

The sign out front is reminiscent of a '50s Wurlitzer jukebox, with artists like The Shirelles, Frankie Lymon and The Teenagers, and Fats Domino. But the real attraction at Bill O'Neill's House of Rock 'n' Roll is the man himself.

Genial and clean-cut, Bill lacks the surly swagger commonly associated with the rock world. Far more archivist than anarchist, Bill is passionate about the music and legacies of those who made it happen. "Just this past year," he explains, "I finally got a couple copies of the first Five Satins 45s on the local New Haven label. That was before they were on Ember, where they had their national success." Right, Bill, the Ember label. Heck, I knew that.

Bill opened his House of Rock 'n' Roll back in the late 1980s after an earlier career as a deejay: "I got fired at twenty-nine, and when I was thirty-eight I asked myself, 'Do I want to get fired again when I'm forty-eight?" Obviously not. Although he's

Hmmm . . . wasn't Rod Stewart with some Brit band back in the sixties? What was their big hit record?

Got questions? Just ask Maine's Rock 'n' Roll answer man.

still on the air part time, it's clear that Bill's "Heart and Soul" is in the House of Rock 'n' Roll. As Bill puts it, "Where else are you going to find all your Ultimate Spinach albums (now re-released on CD)? How about Moby Grape and Peanut Butter Conspiracy? Yup, right over there.

A big part of the fun here lies in picking Bill's brain. He is a virtual encyclopedia of rock trivia. Did you know that Harry Nilsson wrote the Three Dog Night hit "One (Is the Loneliest Number)"? Me neither. The more obscure the artist and label the better he likes it. The very building we are standing in is in a way hallowed ground where the '60s Maine rock band The Id (aka Euphoria's Id on another label) held their rehearsals. One of those 45s today is worth upward of $350. If you're interested in purchasing one, he'll be happy to oblige.

Since I was there anyway, I figured Bill would be just the guy to help me solve a rock 'n' roll mystery that has been bugging me for years. In 1967 Sam & Dave had a big hit with the record "Soul Man." In the song Sam Moore touts his degree in "funkology" by belting out the line "I was educated at Woodstock" I always thought that was a cool lyric until I realized that the song came out two years *before* the famous music festival. So what was the "Soul Man" so hepped up about anyway? I asked Bill. I figured if anybody could clear up the mystery, he could. I figured wrong.

Bill dismissed the whole thing with a laugh. "You just *think* he's saying 'Woodstock,' " said Bill, as if numbskull questions like mine are the inevitable potholes in his daily commute. He went on to explain that some folks are convinced that the Creedence Clearwater song "Bad Moon Rising" includes the lyric "There's a bathroom on the right." Or that Jimi Hendrix pauses in the midst of "Purple Haze" to say, "Excuse me . . . while I kiss this guy." OK, I get the point, Bill. We're not studying the works of Shakespeare here. I must have forgotten: It's just rock 'n' roll.

## RED ARROW SNOWMOBILE CLUB
### St. Agatha

t was 92 degrees in Portland in August when I logged onto the Web site for the town of St. Agatha and the Red Arrow Snowmobile Club. I knew right away was in northern Maine because there was a note to "Click here for local snowmobiling conditions." The next screen had snowflakes coming down, and it reported that, as of March 29, groomer operators from Linneus to Allagash were still reporting excellent trail conditions.

I called Jim Raymond at R&R Snowmobile Repairs in St. Agatha. He works on two or three sleds in the summer months. He says in a typical year the snowmobile trails are good enough to travel on by Thanksgiving, and they are always in good shape through March. Usually there's enough snow to go out the first couple of weeks in April. That's a season of just under six months. The best sledding is in January, but people don't go out then because it's too cold. February brings the big crowds to the "top o' Maine."

The Red Arrow Snowmobile Club has 140 members, which is a sizable number when you consider that the town of St. Agatha has only 900 residents. If the city of Portland had a club with a proportionate membership, there would be about 10,000 members. The club is one of the central features of the town, as it's headquartered next to the town office and firehouse.

The Red Arrow Snowmobile Club takes care of 200 miles of trails, which in turn are connected to another 1,200 miles of snowmobile trails. That's almost the distance from St. Agatha to Portland.

Visitors planning to make a trip to St. Agatha in the winter should book accommodations at least two months in advance. If you are planning to go in the summer, you might have better luck.

When life hands you snow . . . drive
snowmobiles! Better yet, enter them
in a race, like the Red Arrow
Snowmobile Club's annual Snow
Cross event.

The lovely town, originally called Lac A Menon, due to its proximity to Long Lake, is also the site of St. Agatha Historical House, the actual site of the home of Andre Pelletier. (I don't really know who he was.) The house and many properties along Long Lake were the subject of a fierce squatters' rights case in the late 1800s, in which the squatters actually won.

Besides bringing snow machines, snow gear, and legal history books, visitors might brush up on their St. John River "Valley" French. The town Web site wishes you bienvenue.

It also proclaims: "It is common to be greeted by strangers and passersby as you travel through St. Agatha as a welcoming gesture." Again, this is unlike Portland, with its own particular gestures for strangers.

To get to St. Agatha, take Route 162 from Madawaska through Frenchville. Or you can paddle up from Mud Lake to the end of Long Lake. Or, for about half the year, you just get on your snowmobile anywhere in Aroostook County and follow the trails until you get to Snowmobile Route ITS–83, at the end of which you'll find a hot cup of coffee at the Red Arrow Snowmobile Club.

### ROBERT SKOGLUND: IS HE HUMBLE? JUST ASK HIM!
#### St. George

How humble is the Humble Farmer? Well, you'll have to draw your own conclusions. Here's what I can tell you. The Humble Farmer, whose absolutely unaffected, natural Down East drawl has been drifting across the airwaves of Maine Public Radio for more than twenty years now, is actually Robert Skoglund, humorist, after-dinner speaker, jazz musician, educator, radio host, and native of St. George.

I've know Bobby for a quarter of a century now, and I still haven't figured out the humble part. On the one hand, he has a penchant for self-promotion that would put even the most fanatical Amway salesman to shame. On the other hand, he is so dry and off-the-wall and his tongue is always so firmly planted in his cheek that it's hard to believe he ever takes himself or his career, or you or me or anything else, very seriously.

For example, the printed introduction Bobby provides for his after-dinner speaking work includes the following:

*At present [Mr. Skoglund] employs 75,000 workers on his large farm. . . . They live in three hives.*

*Last fall, Humble spoke at a Democratic convention in Augusta—he was hired by Republicans.*

*We have two reasons for bringing Humble here tonight. One, we don't have much time, and he always forgets about half of what he has to say. Two, when we put this job out to bid, he was the only applicant who offered to pay us.*

I first became aware of Humble (This is how he refers to himself. When answering the phone, his first utterance is always "Humble hee-ah!") back in the mid-1970s. I was just one of hundreds (well, perhaps dozens is more like it) of *Maine Times* readers who scoured the Personals each week. We weren't looking for a date, you understand. We were looking for one of Bobby's witty lonely hearts listings. I called him the other day and told him I wanted to put him in my book, and he graciously agreed to supply me with about fifty pounds of promotional material (he just happened to have it lying around). Now, there's a really helpful, humble guy for you.

Among the treasures he sent me were these ads from a quarter century back. (Only a truly humble man saves his old personal ads from two decades back, right?) Here are some of my favorites:

*July '77—Antiques dealer wants to meet attractive young woman interested in one nightstand.*

*December '78—Virile young man wants to meet attractive young woman willing to appear in* Guinness Book of World Records.

*Also December '78—Ornithologist wants to meet attractive young woman willing to sacrifice everything for a few cheep thrills.*

*November '79—Experienced traveler wants to meet attractive young woman who really enjoys being abroad.*

Every now and then one of Bobby's personal ads drew fire for being a bit too risqué. I'm sure he picked up some flak for this one:

*Lonely evangelist seeks attractive young woman eager to assume missionary position in Africa.*

Even the progressive, liberal-minded *Maine Times* flat out refused to print this one:

*Maine trapper seeks attractive lady taxidermist eager to mount four skins.*

At this point, the single women among you will probably be relieved to learn that after fifty-four years as a confirmed bachelor, Bobby finally got hitched. According to Skoglund, he and his long-suffering wife, Marsha (whom he refers to fondly both on his radio show and in his monologues as "The Almost Perfect Woman"), have a very good marriage. You might wonder what charms Marsha employed to lure the Humble Farmer to the altar after so many years of confirmed (and judging from those ads, anyway, presumably very interesting) bachelorhood.

According to Bobby, it wasn't anything all that exotic: "I married her for her health insurance."

*Babe hit the pitch
and the ball went
that-a-way over
that flagpole!*

## *GOODALL PARK*
### *Sanford*

The national pastime is Maine's passion. Baseball is played in cow pastures (be careful sliding into third base!), in back fields, and behind schools, where fans sit in rickety bleachers outside in the fickle elements of weather. There is probably no more beautiful setting for the game than at Goodall

Park in Sanford, a covered field with 786 individual seats and a history that few parks can match.

The park was originally built, in stages, in the early part of the twentieth century by workers at the Goodall Mills, the town's major employer. It was always a covered facility, but there originally were benches or bleachers for the fans. The stands were destroyed by fire in 1997; after receiving enormous community support, the new structure was completed in 1999, at a cost of $1.6 million.

*The seats are 1 inch narrower than the standard. Sit in these and you'll know if you put on a few pounds last winter.*

Blaine Jack, the park's unofficial historian, says the 786 new, individual seats were fit in the stands by making them an inch narrower than the standard 20-inch seats. There are also bench seats for 150 more. Dugouts are actually dug out, and there is a large press box on the third level. With night lighting, Goodall Park is ready for lots of baseball.

The park appears larger than its seating capacity. It's 419 feet to the flag pole in center field, 370 to left, and 295 to right, taking away the right-handed advantage provided by Fenway Park's Green Monster. The fences in the outfield do not have advertising, which provides a somewhat more pristine view of the action. And the field itself is immaculately maintained. Jack said that visiting coaches of collegiate teams have assumed that this was a minor league professional park.

It's the history, though, that makes Goodall Park stand out. The semiprofessional teams of the early twentieth century battled it out here. One special day, the park etched its name forever in Maine baseball history. October 4, 1919, saw a record crowd watch the Sanford Professionals play the Boston Red Sox. As the headline in the *Sanford Tribune* said, the Sanford nine played "gilt-edged baseball," but the visitors prevailed on the strength of a three-run home run by Babe Ruth. The Bambino knocked the ball out of the park. The locals, though losers, were not disappointed: "It was a grand good game to watch," said the *Tribune,* "and many watched it—the biggest paid attendance of the season for the stores and mills were closed for the occasion." When Ruth made an error in the fourth inning, one fan remarked, "G'wan, you lout, get in there and play baseball. What d'yer spose I paid a quarter for your pictures for, anyway?"

All good things must pass. Despite Babe's ability in Sanford, the Red Sox traded him away, leaving the legendary "Curse of the Bambino" on both the Red Sox and their home, Fenway Park. The Goodall Mills closed in the 1950s, leaving just a name on its ballfield. The tragic fire at Goodall Park in 1997 destroyed the stands, old box scores, memorabilia, and a wooden statue of Babe Ruth. But today Goodall Park is open for baseball once again, day and night, proud of its memories and looking forward to the next magic moment when a future star will knock the ball out of the park.

## BABE'S STORE
### Sanford

The magic day when Babe Ruth and the Red Sox came to Sanford in October 1919, the entire town turned out to greet the team. Marching bands escorted the Beantown Boys to Goodall Park, where the stands overflowed with fans

*Whether it's true or not, the legend lives on.*

who shouted with joy when Babe Ruth knocked a huge home run past the outfield fence.

The ball, it is said, went all the way out of the park and smacked into a small building in a nearby field. The building later became a store, and, because of its important place in local lore, it acquired the inevitable moniker, Babe's Store.

Not true, says Lionel Perrault of Sanford. And he ought to know, since he owns the store. The building housing Babe's Store is located more than a football field away from the baseball park, which would make the Babe's homer longer than any in the record books. And the building wasn't even there when the ball was hit.

Most importantly, however, it was Lionel's father, Esdras Perrault, who started the store in 1941. Esdras, who was the youngest in his family, was always called "Babe." It was Babe Perrault who created his eponymous shop, selling sodas, beer, cigarettes, cat food, and little necessary items. Babe's son Lionel took over the business in the mid-1960s.

Of course, these facts have not bothered the mythmakers. Inside Babe's Store, you'll find a ball autographed by Babe Ruth's daughter, who came to town when Goodall Park was rededicated. And Lionel will tell you about how a high school student, doing a history project, had repeated the myth of Babe's Home Run being the basis for the store's name. Lionel told the student that this was not true. He then received a call from the girl's teacher, who told him to shut up and mind his own business. "They didn't want the truth to get in the way of a good story," Lionel says with a smile.

*A store sign in Sanford. Since our worst problem is procrastination, we think we'll make that call later . . . much later!*

# THE EXECUTION STATE?

**M**aine and Texas have some things in common: They border other countries, their people talk kinda funny, and they have a lot of NRA members. One thing thay differ on, though, is the death penalty. Texas can boast of having a seemingly unquenchable thirst for executions, but Maine was the site of the first official execution.

It was in June 1790 that Thomas Bird, a sailor who had been convicted of the federal crimes of piracy and the murder of his captain, swung from the gallows in Portland. Bird had been a sailor on a slave ship off the coast of Africa. He had had an awful childhood, and his lawyers asked President George (Washington, that is) for mercy, but it was to no avail. A crowd of more than 3,000 (more than the entire population of the town) gathered at the execution site on Bramhall Square. The square was quite distant from the main part of town, but it afforded ample space for the crowd to watch the spectacle.

Bird admitted that he had lived a wicked life and had sinned mightily, but he denied actually killing the captain. It didn't matter. He was hanged, and the crowd was happy.

The hanging was the first to occur in the newly constituted United States of America. Texas wasn't even part of the country then. Of course, Maine was part of Massachusetts at the time, but we still get the credit. It was reported that pieces of the gallows were found more than a century later when the Maine Eye and Ear Infirmary was built. Now a marker at the Bramhall Fire Station commemorates the event.

Maine's taste for execution eventually soured. On November 21, 1885, Daniel Wilkinson was hanged at the state prison in Thomaston for the crime of killing a police officer. The newspaper reports of the hanging noted that the death was slow and gruesome. Perhaps if it had occurred in Texas this would have been cause for joy among politicians. But the Maine legislature determined that there were other means of punishment, and the death penalty was abolished in 1887.

The death penalty had been questioned before in Maine after someone stepped forward to confess a crime for which another person had already been executed. This was in the days before DNA. The equivalent penalty in Maine today is a life sentence without parole. Some politicians are grumbling about the need to reinstate the death penalty for particular crimes, but their arguments aren't getting very far. We've been there, done that. If you want an execution, put on your Stetson and mosey on down to Texas.

## *ROGER'S SUPA DOLLA*
### *Sanford*

It's just a grocery store, but the name says a lot about how Mainers adapt to things. I imagine there was a guy named Roger. He wanted to have a 1950s-type "supermarket," where the "dollar" was king. Before he put up the sign, he tested the name on friends and family, using the spelling from forty-nine other states; but everyone pronounced it by dropping the "ER." Why didn't Roger stick to the "proper" spelling? Probably because his name was Roger and he didn't want to put on airs. Or maybe, in true Yankee fashion, he knew that he could save on sign costs by eliminating a few letters. Another store that could consider the naming and cost factors is Rent-A-Center. After all, everyone in Maine calls it "Renta-Centa," so why not just adapt and make things easier?

*This sign is missing a couple of Ahhh's.*

## MEET LENNY, THE CHOCOLATE MOOSE
### Scarborough

For reasons I've never fully understood, catching a glimpse of a moose seems to be at or near the top of a lot of folks' short list of things-to-do-while-we're-in-Maine. Although most natives are apt to have had this experience at least once and can give you suggestions about where and when to look, the likelihood of glimpsing one of these gentle giants in its native habitat is still a long shot.

Fortunately for those visitors with limited time and serious moose-gawking lust, there's always Lenny. Lenny is easy to find, mostly because he never moves. He's located inside the Len Libby Store on Route 1 in Scarborough. In the great tradition of roadside attractions everywhere, Lenny is grandly billed as "the world's largest chocolate moose." That assertion will likely go unchallenged if for no other reason than, as far as anybody can tell, Lenny is the world's *only* life-size chocolate moose sculpture. How big is life-size? Pretty darn big, it turns out. Eight feet tall from the soles of his edible hooves to the tip of his chocoholic's fantasy antlers and, standing in a Maine woods diorama, Lenny looks for all the world like he's apt to turn around and walk out the back door.

*Anybody want dessert?*

*Would you just hurry up and take the picture?*
*My antlers are starting to melt!*

Czechoslovakian sculptor Zdeno Mayercak and his assistants labored for a month to shape this startlingly lifelike quadruped from nearly a ton of pure first-quality Len Libby chocolate, the same handmade delicacy they've been turning out since 1926. I have to admit that when you factor in the beautifully painted Maine woods backdrop, the results are darn impressive. Visitors are encouraged to take snapshots, of course. Hey, come to think of it, if you can manage to snap one that's maybe just a tiny bit out of focus, you might actually convince the folks back home that you were standing 5 feet away from a real, honest-to-goodness Maine moose!

### SKOWHEGAN BIG INDIAN
#### Skowhegan

**M**aine folks like to talk about the importance of being a "native Mainer." The real natives, of course, would dispute the title if applied to someone whose ancestors didn't arrive in Maine until 1600. From that time until fairly recently, those who were here before 1600 were called Indians. Now, as a result of either political correctness or heightened sensitivity, the term Native Americans is used. For example, in Freeport, what was the FBI—the Freeport Big Indian—is now the MBNA—Maine's Big Native American. In Skowhegan, it's still the Indian, and it's a very big one.

The Skowhegan Indian, standing at the intersection of Routes 2 and 201, is 62 feet high and weighs 24,000 pounds. According to the Skowhegan Chamber of Commerce, the Indian was carefully crafted of locally grown white pine by sculptor Bernard Langlais of Cushing. It was a three-year process of planning and assembly, ending in the shipment of the Indian in two pieces to the town. Shirley Whittemore, formerly with the chamber, recalls the day, in 1969, when the Indian arrived, lying on his back with his big feet up in the air.

The original intention of the sponsors of the Indian was to place him in a park, which would include a bandstand and other outdoor amenities. But the wheels of commerce churned differently, and gas stations and businesses surrounded the spot where he stands. Treetops partially obscure the top of the statue. Shirley Whittemore thinks the Indian is out of place now. She'd like to see it closer to, or right at, the Kennebec River. This would fit in with the theme of the Indian as hunter and fisherman (he's holding a spear and a weir net).

Over the years, the Skowhegan Indian has lost some of his color, due to natural aging. The Skowhegan Chamber of Commerce used to hold a cribbage tournament to raise funds to maintain him and keep him free of termites. But he's still in good shape and relatively free from vandals.

What about comments from Native Americans? Shirley Whittemore hasn't heard any negative comments, but she has heard from locals and visitors alike, who think the Indian is ugly or gaudy. She says the sculptor and the sponsors wanted something that resembled the actual features of local Indians. Five models were used in the process of developing a face. The town of Skowhegan, whose sports teams are called the Indians, is proud of its giant Indian, according to Shirley. It draws people to the town, and, she says, it honors the Indians who lived in the area before European settlers and who made peaceful use of local resources.

The Skowhegan Indian was created with attention to detail and color. It is a work of "art," distinct perhaps from other roadside oddities. There are some people, however, for whom all "big art" is in the same category. For these folks, the Skowhegan Indian takes its place along with Paul Bunyan and the Giant Walking Serviceman just as Andrew Wyeth paintings take their place among pictures of kids with big eyes and Elvis on velvet. While everyone agrees it's larger than life, the beholder will have to decide whether the Skowhegan Indian is art, culture, or cultch.

## T HE  C ASTLE
### *South  Freeport*

The Castle in South Freeport is all that remains of a legendary hotel that operated for a dozen years at the beginning of the last century. The Casco Castle was built by the owners of the electric trolley line to promote the line and to get city folks out to the seaside for a 50-cent shore dinner. The hotel had rooms for one hundred guests, spacious grounds,

*The castle tower, a remnant from the early 1900s, looms over the trees. It's a relic from the days of the 50-cent shore dinner.*

and a 300-foot suspension bridge over a ravine at its entrance. The Castle was, at high tide, on its own island. It was a dream, and many old-time Mainers remembered the dream for decades after it was gone.

Fire destroyed the dream that was the Casco Castle. As the *Portland Press* reported on September 9, 1914, "At an early hour yesterday morning that famous summer hotel which because of its unique construction has attracted the attention of summer visitors from all over the country passed up in smoke, fire having raised the structure inside of a half hour." The *Press* went on to report that the proprietor had lost his clothing, a gold watch, and "a valuable bulldog."

The fire was so hot it burned the woodwork from the inside of the stone tower. But the fire did not destroy the tower itself, which gave Casco Castle its charm. The tower, based on a medieval design, remains. It was built of fieldstone, about 100 feet high. There was a staircase going easily to the top, and there were window slits in the sides of the tower, affording visitors views of the surrounding oceanside and countryside. Ships at sea could see the lighted tower and use it as a landmark. (This was before the Big Freeport Indian, which can be seen from the British Isles.)

Trolley service continued to Freeport until 1929, but the tower was not a public attraction. Today, it is privately owned and not open to the public. The view of the castle from South Freeport isn't particularly good. However, you can get a good, unobstructed view of it from Winslow Park, which is the town park in South Freeport. Hikers in Wolfe's Neck State Park can also get a good look at it. Or if you're by the Haraseeket River, you can see what it looks like, and imagine what it looked like, from the water, with the moonlight drenching the gardens and lawns and the band playing "In the Good Old Summertime."

## Fun with Tourists
### Southport Island

His face has the authentic weather-beaten patina you'd expect to see on a man who has spent most of his ninety-plus years on or near the sea. The twinkle in his eyes and his wry grin are an open invitation to unsuspecting tourists. "Come on over," they seem to say. "Set right down. Go ahead . . . ask me a question." Not that Eliot Winslow will do or say anything untoward, mind you. He's not going to bite you or anything. It's just that after having spent several decades being asked the same questions over and over, Eliot's answers have been honed to a fine, dry, Down East edge. Asking Eliot one of the half dozen questions a hundred folks before you have already asked is a bit like lobbing a softball over the plate to Babe Ruth. He'll hit it right out of the ballpark every time.

Eliot's career on the Maine waterfront in and around Boothbay Harbor is a colorful one that spans most of the last century. Among other things, Eliot's a real honest-to-gawd sea captain with the expertise to confidently pilot vessels a good deal longer than the block you live on back home. Don't let the rumpled trousers, scuffed dock shoes, and khaki work shirt fool you. Eliot Winslow is a smart, powerful, and successful man. That tugboat with the big *W* on the stack tied up next to the lobster wharf where you stopped for lunch belongs to him. As a matter of fact, the wharf itself and the restaurant belong to him, too. You wouldn't know it to look at him, but Eliot has made, and well into his nineties continues to make, a very prosperous living for himself around these parts.

Never mind all that, though. To the average tourist who stops by Robinson's Wharf just across the Southport Bridge on Southport Island, Eliot's just another old geezer "numbin'" (his term) around the dock. If you're naive enough to buy that image, you've set yourself up for a good helping of "native wit" from a master of the genre.

By way of example, here's just one funny incident from Eliot's long career. A few summers back Eliot was tidying up in front of the restaurant when he noticed a carload of confused tourists talking among themselves, pointing in various directions, and waving a well-worn road map around. They drove off only to reappear and go through the same routine about a half hour later. According to Eliot, it took them the better part of an hour to make it back to the same spot for a third time, at which point they were ready for some native roadside assistance. Eliot, of course, was more than happy to oblige.

"Are you tryin' to get off Southport Island?" asked Eliot. They acknowledged that they were. "Are you tryin' to get off Southport Island by drivin' west?" Again they answered in the affirmative. "There's your trouble!" he said. "You can't get off

Southport Island by drivin' west." He added helpfully, "If you do that, you'll be the first ones that've ever done it. If you want to get off this island," he advised, "you're going to have to go east, right back across the same bridge you drove across to get onto the island in the first place."

"But we didn't drive across a bridge," said the driver.

"You mean to tell me you didn't drive across no bridge to get onto Southport Island?" asked Eliot.

"That's right," said the tourist.

"Well, in that case," Eliot replied, "I take back what I said before. Your trouble is . . . you ain't here yet!"

Eliot swears this incident really happened, and, having grown up in Maine, I tend to believe him. But, true or not, it's a great story, and when you're talking to a real Maine geezer, that's pretty much the whole point.

## CAN A FUNNY STORY SAVE A LIFE?
### *Stonington*

Stonington, located on the southern tip of Deer Isle, is a picture-book example of a Maine fishing village. I once heard an old-timer remark, "Stonington was the last place on earth that God made. Then the Almighty went and decided to put salt water around it so it wouldn't freeze up."

I can't comment on that, but I do know that, for better or worse, richer or poorer, in sickness and in health, folks in Stonington have been virtually married to the sea for many generations.

A few years back, in response to the tragic deaths at sea of two young island fishermen, Sue Oliver decided to start an organization. Along with other local women, mostly fishermen's wives (and daughters and sisters, too), she founded the nonprofit Island Fishermen's Wives Association. Of the

*172*

organization, Sue says, "We try to raise funds for several different causes. If a fisherman dies or loses a boat, we try to help out the family." One of the first projects Sue and the other wives completed was a fishermen's memorial on the waterfront in Stoningon. The hope was that when the fishermen passed the monument on their way to work on the open sea, they would be reminded to "be safe, have the right equipment on their boats, like that . . . do the right thing."

One of the most popular fund-raisers for the group in recent years has been the Fishermen's Wives Storytelling Contest. "We did it in January," says Sue, "so it was all local people." She added with a laugh, "No one comes here in January!" The event, held at the Island Center, was the result of Sue's attending a similar event at a waterfront bar in Boothbay Harbor, where she remembers hearing the following:

"This woman got up, and she was telling a story about this guy who'd gone to Nova Scotia to pick up a boat. On his way back, he went below to take a nap, and he took his teeth out and left them to soak in a glass of water." According to the tale, the man's shipmates decided to play a practical joke on him by replacing the water with 90 proof rum. Sue continues, "Then they got worried that the rum would rot the dentures. But they figured 'Hey, the way he drinks, if they're not rotten by now, this won't hurt 'em any!' So when he got up in the morning, he took out the teeth, shook 'em a bit, put 'em in, and made a major face." Examining the glass, the sailor is said to have commented "It's a shame to waste good rum like that." Whereupon he added a bit of Coke and proceeded to drink his breakfast.

Although that story got a laugh out of Sue, she's dead serious about the work of her organization. "If we can save even one life, it will be more than worth it," she says. A recent Fishermen's Wives event may well have done just that. "We had the guys get in their survival suits, jump overboard, and swim to a raft. One guy got into his suit, jumped overboard, and discovered that it was full of holes. He almost drowned right in front of us all." After that embarrassing episode, Sue says that the chagrined sailor "got out of water, took off the suit, and threw it in the trash."

Perhaps that one incident, tragedy averted by a little good-spirited razzing, could serve as a kind of mission statement for the work of the Island Fishermen's Wives Association. What they seem to be saying is "A little laughter now can save a lot of tears later on."

## THE PRISON STORE: SHOPLIFTERS WILL BE PROSECUTED IMMEDIATELY!
### *Thomaston*

A s any merchant in America will tell you, shoplifting is a major headache and a tremendous financial burden for businesses, particularly small operations such as gift shops. Interestingly enough, one of the busiest gift shops on the Maine coast, a modest storefront operation on Main Street in Thomaston, has no such problems. Despite the fact that many of the items on sale are small and easily pocketed by "light-fingered Louies," manager Joe Allen assures us that with a half million customers a year, pilferage is simply not a problem. He goes on to speculate that perhaps the uniformed guards patrolling the aisles may have something to do with it. Then again, it's very possible that the sales staff, a half dozen or so inmates from the Maine State Prison next door, create a certain "crime doesn't pay" ambience.

*Need a sign? No problem, Warden.*

The Maine State Prison Showroom, commonly referred to as the "prison store," has been doing a brisk business in downtown Thomaston since the Great Depression. The merchandise consists of high-quality furniture and handcrafted novelty items built by inmates in the prison workshop. They're not working for 10 cents an hour, either. The inmates in the program design their own projects and essentially run a small manufacturing business behind bars. Each inmate is allowed by law to earn a maximum of $10,000 per year (gross). Proceeds from their work often go to make restitution to victims of their crimes or to help support their families on the outside.

There is something a little strange about buying items made and sold by prisoners. A lot of folks notice that the original crafts projects tend to have an ironic twist. For example, the name of the wooden schooner model for sale in the showroom window, *Freedom's Way,* makes it hard to forget exactly where and by whom the vessel was built. Parking for the prison store is located out back. To keep you from blocking the loading ramp, the prisoners made a sign reading LOADING ZONE. PARKED VEHICLES WILL BE TOWED. How can you tell that the sign was made by prisoners? Each word is printed on its own individual license plate! Hey, at least they aren't doing time in New Hampshire, where all the plates stamped out by the inmates read LIVE FREE OR DIE.

## I'VE BEEN MEANING TO STOP BY MOODY'S DINER
### Waldoboro

If you randomly stopped fifty Mainers on the street and asked whether they'd ever been to Moody's Diner on coastal Route 1 in Waldoboro, most likely forty-eight of them would say they had and the other two would say they'd been meaning to, but there's always a long line of folks waiting to get in. What is it

*When you start out with a good idea . . .*

that makes Moody's such a Maine landmark, anyway? When I called recently to pose that very question to owner/manager Nancy Moody Genthner, granddaughter of Percy Moody, who founded the wildly popular eatery back in the 1920s, I was told that she would be happy to discuss the matter, but it might be several hours before she could call me back. It seems there's quite a line right now and she's kinda busy. Big surprise.

Meanwhile, here's what I already know. Stepping in the front door at Moody's Diner (once you've made it through that almost inevitable waiting line) is like stepping back in time. Moody's isn't a nostalgic remake of anything. Moody's Diner is the culinary arts version of the old line "If it ain't broke, don't fix it." You see that ancient faded linoleum countertop? The one with the ruts worn in it from generations of customers sliding the salt, pepper, sugar, and ketchup back and forth twenty-four hours a day? That's Moody's Diner! How about the waitress who can probably recall the day she served President Taft a third slice of pie and can definitely reel off a list of about forty homemade desserts in a tenth of the time it takes you to decide? That's Moody's Diner!

And if you're thinking you'll beat the rush and stop by late at night when things are slow, better think again. That trademark orange-and-green hand-lettered MOODY'S sign with the neon trim is, to the weary traveler, what a porch light is to a moth. Ayuh, Moody's just plain draws 'em in. But, by all means, if you get the chance, stop by. It'll be an experience you won't soon forget. Once you've scarfed down a hot open-faced pork sandwich topped off with a cup of coffee and a slice of homemade pie, you too will be telling all your friends that you've eaten at Moody's Diner. And when they say "I've been meaning to do that, but every time I drive by the place is packed," at least you'll finally know why.

*. . . folks will beat a path to your door.*

*Whoever runs this place has certainly figured out who his target market is.*

*I suppose that the older you get the harder it is to pass up bargains like this one.*

# TRANSPORTATION TRIVIA

*Did You Know?*

1. *Shortest numbered highway route in Maine: Route 217 in Phippsburg from Route 209 to Sebasco Estates. (Why bother to give it a number?)*

2. *Widest roads in the state of Maine:*

   *a. Maine Street in Brunswick. At 101 feet, it is almost as wide as Route 217 is long. With the traffic so heavy in the busy downtown area of Brunswick, it also provides exciting adventures should one decide to try crossing the street. Maine Street in Brunswick is so wide that when there is a parade, some schools can line their entire marching bands up in one row across.*

   *b. Route 1, Mars Hill. Downtown Mars Hill, with its 82-foot-wide Main Street, resembles a western cow town. Cars can easily park at an angle to the curb, and there is plenty of space for four lanes of cars (if there are that many in town at one time). Perhaps the street is so wide because it marks the confluence of two big roads—Route 1, going west toward Presque Isle, and Route 1A, going north toward Fort Fairfield. The town's wide street is made famous in the book* Women Who Come from Mars Hill and the Men Who Eat Venison.

   *c. Commercial Street, Portland: There is so much trafffic—foot, auto, and formerly rail—that one forgets how wide it is (82 feet). This street was built on filled land over the edge of Portland Harbor and designed for ship commerce. Now the commerce comes not only from fishing and trade but also from tourist ships and big buses. Quaint cobble and paving stones make this an attractive feature of the Old Port area, which, in turn, places Commercial Street at the center of the battleground for the future of Portland's waterfront—a battle between those who want to keep their lobster traps and those who want to create a tourist trap.*

3. *Places where you can go south on a northbound road: We think that the interstate system was designed to get us there faster, and*

the quickest way to get there from here is by means of a straight line. We would assume, therefore, that if we were headed north on Interstate 95, we would always be heading generally in a northerly direction. It's not always so. If you have a compass in your vehicle, take a look at the reading the next time you're heading from Newport to Bangor—yup, it's southerly, or southwesterly. Look at it on the map. It comes awful close to doing the same thing just outside Houlton, and it clearly does take a southerly dip as it approaches the border crossing. Of course, who could blame you for wanting to take a southerly dip in Houlton?

4. *Northernmost numbered highway point:* Entrance on Route 1 to the bridge between Madawaska and Edmunston, New Brunswick. Route 1 is all downhill—both east and west—from there. This bridge is famous for the thousands of people who come to Maine from Canada to buy lower priced cigarettes, and the hundreds of Mainers who go to Canada to buy lower priced prescription drugs.

5. *Northernmost highway point:* A logging road appears to run out of Big Twenty Township, the northernmost township in Maine (known to its friends as T20, R11 & R12, WELS). The road runs into Canada and then along the border for a bit until it comes upon the Customs Office in Estcourt, Quebec, but arguably on U. S. soil. This section of the map of Maine is usually in a separate section, like Alaska and Hawaii appear on a map of the United States. Most of us will never go there (why would we?), but it is comforting to know that it's there.

6. *Highest elevation on the state highway system:* Height of Land on Route 17, in Township D, on the back road between Rumford and Rangeley. Route 17 is a beautiful road, although it is bumpy and potholed in places in summer and completely impassable at times in winter. You are likely to see a moose in one of the lower level ponds. At its highest point, the Appalachian Trail crosses the road. When you look out over the surrounding hills and valleys, you won't think you are in Maine, but rather in the mountainous terrain of the western United States. One other thing: To many Mainers, this is the "heighth of land."

### GROAN & McGURN TOURIST TRAP
#### West Bethel

When visitors "from away" poke their heads into the store called Groan & McGurn's Tourist Trap, in West Bethel, they often say, "We just had to see what a tourist trap really looks like." They might be greeted with the answer, "They're really not too hard to find; there's about a million of them on the highways of Maine."

The Tourist Trap started out in 1966 as the L&F Country Store. Eric Paul, whose parents owned the store, started selling T-shirts in the store in the late 1970s. Eric also traded T-shirts at craft shows for the goods made by potters and other craftspeople. He then sold the bartered craft items in the store. When the country store closed, the Tourist Trap opened up. Groan & McGurn were two of Eric's cats, and their names grace the establishment.

Initially, Eric said, the store sold "a lot of high-end stuff. My T-shirts were the trashiest items." Gradually, the focus of store items was on stuffed animals and refrigerator magnets—stuff the tourists like to get trapped into buying. Now, there's a lot of good stuff, mostly new, but some used, some treasures, some kitsch. As Eric says, "It's entertaining to look at and wonderful to own."

Among the maps, coffee cups, bells, and spoons that one would expect to find in a tourist trap, the store has a plastic cigar store Indian and plastic Laurel and Hardy lifesize figures. The figures look so real, Eric says, that one time a state trooper was prepared to shoot at them, thinking they were intruders. When he gets too much stuff in the store, Eric has an auction to clean out the old and to make room for the new.

The busiest time of year for the Tourist Trap is summer, as it is on the coast, although the "leaf peepers" have extended the season. People come in for directions to Canada or to Old

Orchard Beach, both locations a far piece from Bethel. Eric doesn't mind giving directions, even accurate ones, because his favorite pastime is shooting the breeze with the folks he has trapped. Some people may drive by the sign, thinking it is the worst form of advertising there could be. But many more folks come to a screeching halt on Route 2 and step inside for the experience of truth in advertising.

## THE GIANT WALKING SERVICEMAN
### *Westbrook*

In the days when big people ruled the earth, there was only one person who could fix their big TVs and stereos—the Giant Walking Serviceman. Standing at the corner of Route 302 and Duck Pond Road in Westbrook, this cultural icon has been a Maine landmark for forty years.

The serviceman was built by Al Hawkes, who, with his father, owned a TV and radio sales and repair shop. Al was inspired by the big neon and fluorescent moving signs of the late 1940s. For example, he said, "There was a laundry in Portland that had a scrubwoman on a sign; her arms were always moving." After hiring a local artist to design the man, Al took a course in welding and hired Morin's wrecking company to put the pipes in the ground. Then he commenced to weld. It took him, his father (who was also a high school teacher), and a high school kid more than six months' worth of nights and weekends to weld and assemble the statue. Al set 385 lightbulbs and additional fluorescent lighting in a circular pattern on the sign. He got a mechanical motor to move the arm back and forth as it hefted a box of TV tubes and equipment. And he put a lot of fuses in the machinery: "That way, if something went out, I could pinpoint the problem instead of taking the whole thing apart."

When he flipped the switch, sometime in 1962, it started up perfectly. The lights gleamed, the arm moved, and the man started a constant motion. In fact, people thought he was walking. But he wasn't.

"We had a contest one time, and we asked, 'How many miles has that serviceman walked over the course of its existence?' The answer was—it hasn't walked an inch." People were furious, and they insisted that it was walking. They were wrong. The only moving part was the arm; the rest, including the walking, was an illusion.

One cold winter day, it got just too cold for the poor old fella. "I got a call from the owner of the store across the street. He said, 'Your man is smoking.' I said, 'Well, he's old enough.' And he said, 'No, really. Smoke is coming up from his shoulders.' " It had been a very cold day, and they hadn't used the right oil on the man's moving arm. The motor kept going and burned out the bearings. A new one-horsepower motor, with heavier duty oil, soon made things right.

*Does he make house calls? I hope not!*

In his heyday, the man was lit up until about 10:00 or 11:00 each evening, with light sensors getting him started and timers making sure he had a rest. The electric bill for running the guy started adding up to close to two hundred bucks a month. He became too high-maintenance for the business.

When the store closed and the billboard laws (applied to busy roads like Route 302) became more restrictive, the walking days of the serviceman were numbered. He became somewhat shopworn. But there are true art lovers everywhere. In the fall and winter of 2000, some neighbors restored the facade of the man. They put up staging and primed and painted him. They replaced his lightbulbs (although they aren't turned on anymore), and they sent him on his way for another forty years of guarding the road.

"The day I take this guy down, I'll have an instant death," says Al. "A lot of people have told me this is the only point of direction they can give people to get to their place, and without it, we'd all be lost." This is true, even if solid state has replaced the tubes in the case. We'd all be lost without the Giant Walking Serviceman.

### JOE PERHAM, MAINE STORYTELLER
#### West Paris

A lot of classroom teachers are comedian wanna-bes, dreaming of the day when they can ditch the routine of the classroom and take their routine on the road. Fortunately for audiences around the country, former Maine English teacher Joe Perham has done just that. Joe retired a few years back and took up entertaining full time. I say fortunately because Joe is a seriously funny guy with a professionally honed native wit, which inevitably leaves his audiences weak from laughter.

Joe has cranked out no fewer than fifteen storytelling tapes of Maine humor, has appeared in films including *Graveyard Shift* and *Bed and Breakfast,* and has recorded numerous radio and TV spots. He has also appeared onstage in the persona of legendary nineteenth-century Maine humorist Artemis Ward (the pen name of humorist Charles Farrar Brown of Waterford, Maine). Brown speaking in his A. Ward character was a favorite of both Abe Lincoln and Mark Twain. Perham has also appeared as Holman Day, famous turn-of-the-twentieth-century Maine poet, author, and early filmmaker.

*Joe Perham, Master Maine Storyteller.*

Joe Perham hails from West Paris, just down the road from the Trap Corner Store, which features prominently in his monologues. He has found his niche in the pantheon of great Maine storytellers by specializing in stories about hunting and fishing. In addition to his amusing tales from the Maine woods, Joe is a virtual encyclopedia of classic New England privy or outhouse jokes.

His seemingly endless supply of funny lines are delivered in a natural Down East accent. But he's anything but laconic. His snappy, rapid-fire style barely lets you recover from the last line before you have to laugh at the next. You never know exactly where Joe is headed, and that's a big part of the fun. Here's an example of one of my favorite Joe Perham lines:

*"I come from a family of fourteen kids. . . . I never slept alone 'til I was married!"*

See what I mean? Joe has graciously agreed to supply the following Top Ten Maine Outhouse Jokes. In no particular order, they are as follows:

1. A Texas senator was invited to visit some Maine businesses. Speaking from atop a farmer's manure spreader, he announced, "This is the first time I've ever been asked to speak from the Republican platform." Touring a clothespin mill, he was heard to say, "Work done on too small a scale. You got to think big to compete." The mill owner takes him to view the inventory building. "Take a look, Senator," he says. "This building has eight doors. That big enough for ya?" "Heck," says the senator, "We got outhouses in Texas bigger than this!" The mill owner replies dryly, "I guess you prob'ly need 'em, too!"

2. A father gets home late, goes upstairs to say good night to his son, and finds him kneeling behind the bed. To set a good example, he gets down on his knees and starts to pray, too. The boy says, "What are you doing, Dad?" The father replies, "Same thing you are, son." The boy says, "Mom is going to be awfully mad. There's only one pot in here!"

3. On a Maine farm, after fall cleaning, Grammie pours liquid naphtha down the privy hole. Grampa goes out there, sits a spell, lights his pipe, and drops a burning match down the hole. An explosion results. Grampa says (pick one): A. "I'm glad I didn't try to sneak that one out in the kitchen!" B. "It must'a been somethin' I 'et!" After this incident, Grampa installs brass handles on the seat to help hold himself down if it ever happens again.

4. This heavy fella goes into an outhouse at a Maine fairground late one evening. As he sits down, the seat gives way, dropping him 7 feet below. He starts hollering, "Fire! Fire!" A crew of firemen arrives shortly and hauls him out. The fire

chief asks, "How come you hollered, 'Fire!'?" To which the
heavyset man replies, "How many people you think would'a
showed up if I'd hollered what I was really into?"

5. The morning after Halloween, a father asks his son if he
knows who pushed over the family privy the night before,
reminding the boy how George Washington confessed to
cutting down the cherry tree. The boy admits that he and his
friend were the culprits, and his dad proceeds to "whale the
tar" out of him. The kid cries, "When George Washington told
the truth, he didn't get a lickin'. How come I did?" His dad
says, "When George Washington cut down the cherry tree,
his father wasn't sitting in it. That's how come!"

6. A woman from rural Maine, having lived her life serviced by
an old-fashioned privy, finally moves into a new home
equipped with a "water closet," an early commode popular in
New England. She writes to her son, "Our new home has a
washing machine, but it don't work too good. I put in
fourteen shirts, pulled the chain, ain't seen the shirts since! It
had two lids on it; I used one for a breadboard. The other one
had a hole in it, so I used it to frame Grampa's pitcha."

7. A man put a fresh coat of varnish on the toilet seat in his
outhouse, but he forgot to put a sign on the door. His wife
went in, locked the door, and settled in. When she tried to get
up, she couldn't. Her husband had to break down the door,
unhook the seat, and carry her into the doctor's office with
the seat still attached. The nurse said, "Ever seen a sight like
that, Doc?" He replied, "Yes, but this is the first time I've ever
seen one framed!"

8. Fred and Ed were out hunting. Fred went behind a bush to
seek some relief and sat right down on a bear trap that was
chained to the bush. At the hunting camp later, Ed said, "The
sound that came out of Fred was the second loudest noise I
ever heard in my life." Someone asked,"The second loudest?"
Ed says, "Yeah, the first loudest noise I ever heard was when
Fred hit the end of that chain!"

9. Maine selectmen traditionally have had buildings equipped
   with a two-hole outhouse. Occasionally town folk have
   suggested that it would be more appropriate if they had a
   one holer so that the selectmen wouldn't be forced to make a
   decision. Some even suggested a one-half holer—for what
   reason we can only surmise.

10. Selectmen's duties often involve inspecting privies. There's a
    tale of one selectman who informed a woman that she'd have
    to move her privy because it was "too close to running
    water." She says, "Who are you to tell me what to do?" He
    says, "I'm the privy inspector." She says, "Good. I'm having
    trouble with my privy." He says, "What's the problem?" She
    says, "You're the privy inspector. You tell me." So he checks
    the structure, outside and in, going so far as to stick his
    head down inside the hole. As he pulls his head out, his
    beard gets caught in a crack in the seat. He hollers, "Ouch,
    my beard's caught! I'm stuck!" To which she responds,
    "Irritatin', ain't it?"

## PAINTING THE BARTER FAMILY TREE
### West Sullivan

In a state known for its artists, Philip Barter is a real breath
of fresh air. His paintings, sculptures, carvings, and wildly
original furniture seem almost alive. Full of brilliant colors
and playful forms, Phil's creations are bursting at the seams
with the pure joy of the visual experience. Philip Barter is a
native Mainer, one of the Boothbay Barters (from Barter's
Island, no less) and darn proud of it. In a recent conversation he
chortled heartily over a piece of historical trivia he'd run across
recently. Phil says that there are rumors around to the effect

that his forebears—the original Barter's Island Barters—may have actually rowed here from England back in the late sixteenth or early seventeenth century. I don't know about that. But if those early Barters had half the energy Phil does, it's certainly possible.

These days you can find Phil, his wife, Priscilla, and a random selection of other Barter family members at the Barter Family Gallery in West Sullivan. The gallery was Phil's idea. After enduring the requisite "starving artist" period, which painters with Phil's talent always seem destined to endure, his work finally started to take off big time back in the late 1980s. A major retrospective of his paintings at Bates College in 1992 solidified his growing reputation as one of the great contemporary Maine painters.

Now, all that acclaim and recognition must have felt good. But keep in mind that Phil came up the hard way. As a Barter from Barter's Island, he certainly appreciated the substantial fees his work was finally bringing in, but chafed at the 50 percent commissions the galleries sliced off the top. That's how he tells it, anyway. Frankly, I think the true motivation behind the Barter Family Gallery is more personal. I just think Phil would rather hang around painting, mentoring, and encouraging his brood of incredibly talented kids than stand around sipping flat Chablis at a stuffy gallery opening.

Whatever the Barters' motivation for starting their enterprise, the gallery itself is not to be missed. It's pretty easy to find, too. Just take Route 1 North out of Ellsworth; after you cross the Hancock/Sullivan Bridge, keep your eyes peeled for a sign that reads BARTER FAMILY GALLERY 2½ MILES. Hang a left, follow the signs along the way, and literally, you can't miss it. The gallery, on the right-hand side of the road, looks more or less like the aftermath of an explosion at a paint factory. Over the years, the Barters have carefully hand-painted nearly every visible surface of the whole rambling structure. Mullions, sills, archways, etc., shimmer in a variety of arresting colors. There are paintings everywhere, inside and out, brilliantly hued sculptures all around the grounds, and wildly painted furniture

*That would be Phil on the left . . . and Phil on the right.*

set about the yard. The whole place has a fanciful fairy-tale quality that just cries out for exploration.

Mostly, Phil and Priscilla are around (if not, just drop a note on the pad by the side of the door), and chatting with them is a huge part of the fun. Although Phil has recently recovered from major surgery (completely successful, he assures me), he has lost none of his zest for life. Whether you end up buying something or not, just poking around the place will give you enough visual stimulation to last you for several weeks.

I know you'll have a good time with the Barter family. But, I must warn you, their creativity is infectious, and side effects may develop. After you've been through the gallery and made your way back home, you're apt to find that the old pine chairs in your living room are suddenly starting to look a little dowdy. That's usually the first symptom. If you catch yourself lingering over paintbrushes and little cans of bright purple, fire engine red, and lemon yellow high-gloss enamel, you can be pretty sure that you've caught the "Barter bug." If you're as lucky as Phil, you'll find that it's incurable.

*B A B B ' S   B R I D G E*
*W i n d h a m*

**W**hen I was a lad, my friends and I went to Babb's Bridge,
a covered bridge that spans the Presumpscot River
between Windham and Gorham. We jumped off its
lower trusses into the Presumpscot. Some brave souls jumped
from the roof of the bridge, others jumped in by means of the
tire swing on the tree next to it. Cars and trucks would beep
their horns as they entered the bridge; then you would hear
their tires thunk on the wooden floor and make the same
crossing that horse-drawn wagons did more than 150 years ago
when the bridge was built. This was as bucolic as you could get,
and it was in the same river that, as it went downstream,
powered mighty paper mills and became a foul sewer as it
flowed into the sea.

The opportunities for swimming might be gone today, but
there's still a covered bridge. By car, or horse, just go north on
River Road toward North Windham. About 1½ miles after the
intersection with Route 202, turn left at the sign and go about
another ½ mile to Babb's Bridge.

There you'll find Babb's Bridge, a replica of the original,
which had been built in 1864 using the Howe truss method of
construction. (This was either a method of construction or
something the workers who carried the heavy beams had to
wear.) Upon entering the structure (beep first to alert oncoming
traffic) your wheels touch the wooden floor, which is suspended
on a series of "chords," or heavy beams, set parallel to the
roadway. You will notice the post-and-beam construction of the
timbers supporting the roof. It's cozy in there, like being in an
old barn.

There are only eight covered bridges left in Maine, according to the Maine Department of Transportation. There once were 120, but they have been washed away and rotted out. Babb's Bridge and the other covered bridges were constructed to keep the rain and snow off the timbers holding up the bridge and, in many cases, forming the roadway. This reduced the rot and swelling. The remaining bridges have survived for 150 years, so their coverings actually served their noble purpose.

In 1985, the Maine legislature, which recently debated whether to give laptop computers to school-age kids, authorized the Department of Transportation to maintain and preserve

*Admit it, sometimes quaint ain't such a bad thing. Don't forget to beep your horn before you drive onto Babb's Bridge.*

covered bridges that weren't part of the state highway system. Babb's Bridge was doing well keeping out natural elements, but it couldn't withstand the onslaught of humans. In 1973, vandals burned the structure. An "exact replica" was constructed on the site and opened in 1976.

Those less bucolically inclined might wonder why our tax dollars have gone to reconstruct a covered bridge, when a steel and metal and asphalt structure would cost less and be more reliable. Perhaps a cost-benefit analysis was performed, showing that tourists will shell out more money when they have these quaint amenities. Or perhaps it was because we like the old covered bridges and we want to keep a few of 'em around. At any rate, Babb's Bridge should be there for another 150 years, if the vandals keep away and the river doesn't rise too much.

## MAINE'S BIGGEST SMALL EATERY
### Wiscasset

There's no surer sign that tourist season has hit the Maine coast than a swarm of tourists and locals around Red's Eats on an early summer evening. You never know who you're going to run into at Red's. A couple of summers back Tom Cruise hopped out of a stretch limo to pick up some hot dogs and an order of fries to go.

Red's Eats, situated on the western end of the Wiscasset bridge since 1938, is a classic example of the New England Clam Shack school of architecture, and the basic menu is pretty much what you'd expect. Besides burgers and dogs, you've got your french fries, fried onion rings, fried shrimp, fried haddock, fried clams, fried scallops . . . are you beginning to notice a trend here? I haven't checked with the American Heart Association or anything, but it's a safe bet that an average meal at Red's will take care of your maximum daily recommended cholesterol intake for pretty much the rest of the summer.

*Folks drop by Red's for fried everything and celebrity gawking.*

And they're not resting on their laurels, either. The motto at Red's Eats might as well be "When better artery busters are built, we'll build 'em!" Of course, you can't go wrong with the world-famous-since-1938 "sturdly," a grilled hot dog split down the middle and stuffed with American cheese. But if you don't happen to own a bathroom scale and you're feeling lucky today, why not plunge right into Red's latest creation, the aptly named "puff dog," a split wiener, liberally stuffed with bacon and cheese, then rolled in heavy batter and, you guessed it, deep fried.

Are you tired of paying an arm and a leg for a lobster roll with a couple of ounces of lobster and a quarter pound of iceberg lettuce? You came to the right place. Although you may want to check with your broker before treating the family to lobster rolls at Red's, at least nobody will be complaining about the serving size. A few years back, Red (that's owner Al Gagnon, who has been slaving over a hot fry-o-lator at Red's for nearly a quarter of a century) started making his lobster rolls with *"at least,"* he says, "a whole pound of lobster meat in each one!" And the price? "Market price," says Al. That's currently twelve bucks a pop. Maybe a few "sturdlies" would be a more responsible choice, after all. Either way, you'll have fun. Just don't mention this little outing to your cardiologist, OK?

## THE "LOST SCHOONERS" OF WICASSET
### Wiscasset

Hesper and Luther will be missed. For many folks, the little riverside village of Wiscasset just won't be the same without the familiar old salts sitting side by side down by the banks of the Sheepscott. Where did they go? Well, in a sense, like Douglas MacArthur's famous old soldiers, they just "faded away"—and thereby hangs a tale.

The names I just mentioned are not those of venerable senior citizens (although, in some sense, perhaps they might as well be). Nope, Hesper and Luther are (or were) a pair of aging coastal schooners, *The Hesper* and *The Luther Little,* which for the better part of a century sat abandoned in the mudflats at the western end of the Wiscasset bridge.

The hard truth is that the age of sail, that halcyon era when proud, square-rigged schooners crowded the shipping lanes, lines taut, sails billowing, hauling Maine timber, ice, and sardines to distant ports, ended not with a whimper but with a bang—the bang of a steam engine. Almost overnight these graceful wooden-hulled "ladies of the sea" were just plain obsolete, eclipsed by steam-powered vessels, capable of making deliveries on time with or without a stiff breeze.

Up and down the Maine coast, hundreds of these once proud vessels were unceremoniously (and illegally) dumped in the

nearest harbor or along a riverbank. For many they were just a
nuisance and a hazard to navigation. But they were too big to
haul off, and where would you put them, anyway? Who would
pay for the job? So these ships just sat rotting away in the mud,
looking about as romantic to the locals as a pair of abandoned
Chevys rusting on the front lawn.

Fortunately, the tourists saw them in a different light.
Painters and photographers started coming around to capture
their salty essence, Charles Kuralt featured them in one of his
famous "On the Road" stories for CBS News, and before you
knew it, a major tourist attraction had been born. The image of
the abandoned schooners soon became pretty much the official
symbol of Wiscasset.

A restaurant called Le Garage opened on the riverbank. Its
menu featured a sketch of Hester and Luther. It was always a
big deal to get there early enough to claim a choice table
overlooking the hulking barnacle-clad derelicts. Postcards and
note cards and T-shirts emblazoned with the image of the
schooners flooded the town. Even the town seal, reproduced on
official stationery and emblazoned on the doors of local police
cruisers, features Wiscasset's famous senior citizens.

Naturally, you want to go take a look at them, right? Sorry
'bout that! You see, while folks were busy cranking out postcards
and T-shirts and menus and knickknacks of the schooners, the
actual ships themselves were doing the only thing they could do
under the circumstances. They were rotting away.

Mercifully, the end came quickly. Following a particularly
blustery midnight storm back in the mid-1990s, early-morning
commuters, lobstermen headed out to tend their traps, and
everybody else who glanced in their direction got a rude shock.
The schooners, which had sat there for almost a century, were
gone. Just gone.

Don't take it too hard, though. Wiscasset still bears the
ghostly imprint of these famous wrecks, and as long as there
are tourist dollars to be snagged, you'll still be able to buy a nice
set of note cards with a sketch of *The Hester* and *The Luther
Little* on them. There is also one other plus: As you travel

around Maine, you'll notice that the natives have an irritating habit of giving directions based on landmarks that no longer exist. So don't be surprised if, when asking a local for directions to Fort Edgecomb, he says "Drive down to Wiscasset, then cross the bridge right where them old ships used to be . . . ." Call me romantic, but I say there's something kinda comforting in knowing that Mainers will still be using these old salts as a landmark a century or two after they gave up the ghost.

## A MATTER OF "TASTE"
### Woolwich

When Larry Crooker, owner of the Taste of Maine restaurant in Woolwich, first clapped his eyeballs on the giant, bucktoothed lobster welded together from rusty abandoned oil drums, he wasn't particularly pleased at the sight. The odd, oxidizing crustacean simply appeared out of nowhere one Monday morning parked on an abandoned broken down trailer right in the middle of his restaurant parking lot in Woolwich, right in the middle of tourist season. He had no idea how it got there, who it belonged to, or how to remove it. It just sat there being an eyesore and taking up precious tourist parking spots. According to Larry, "It was kinda in the way, and we were wonderin' what it was gonna take to get it outta there."

Over the next few days, however, Larry's attitude began to change. "The people [hungry tourists] kept lookin' at this thing, and we kept lookin' at it, and it kinda grew on us," he says. "After a few days, when he finally came around ["he" being the sculptor Robert Daniels of St. George, Maine, who was towing his creation to an art exhibit in Kittery when a broken trailer axle forced him to abandon it in the restaurant's parking lot], we decided it was kind of an attraction."

The enthusiastic reaction of his customers had expanded Larry's artistic sensibilities considerably. Acting on his newfound "taste" for monumental sculpture, Larry purchased

*I never claimed that Maine lobsters are always in good taste.*
*I just said that they always taste good.*

the lobster for $2,500 on the spot. His own creative spirit now liberated, he set to work "sprucing it up" for its new role as a famous Maine culinary landmark. "My father had some of these big metal buoys they have in the ocean." (Surprised? Don't be. Nobody ever throws anything away in Maine. You never know when it'll come in handy.) "We put them around it. Then we put some lobster traps around it." (Piling old wooden lobster traps on just about anything, from a rusted-out Buick to a granite boulder, is a time-honored marketing technique along Maine's coastal Route 1.) "We had a little sign made that says TASTE OF MAINE on it. Because the people kept gettin' around it takin' pictures of it, we wanted everybody to know where it is." (Natch.) "And then we painted it bright red" (always a good idea with a giant lobster in these parts) "so when you come up over the hill there it kinda hits you right in the eye."

That it does. And when you're trolling for tourist dollars along the Maine coast, "hittin' 'em right in the eye" is what it's all about.

# FOLLOW YOUR "DREMS"

**F**or some reason, the dozen or so miles of coastal Route 1 from the east bank of the Kennebec River in Woolwich to the west bank of the Sheepscott in Wiscasset has, over the years, become a magnet for roadside vendors. It's anybody's guess how this happened, but I think it probably has something to do with traffic congestion. Traditionally, both the Bath bridge and the one in Wiscasset have been notorious summertime bottlenecks. Despite the DOT's best efforts to move things along (both bridges have been widened in recent years), you might just as well accept the fact that you'll be doing a lot of idling, downshifting, and gawking on this particular stretch between July 4 and Labor Day.

That's OK. This is Maine, remember? Life in the slow lane? Depending on the time of year, you're going to have plenty of opportunities to stop and purchase a dizzying array of products, from fresh farm produce to homemade handcrafts to discounted designer jeans as you crawl inexorably toward your final destination. Take the right attitude and this ribbon of bumper to bumper, two-lane Maine blacktop might just be the ultimate cure for road rage. You might as well relax. Ain't NOBODY goin' anywhere fast on this road today.

Meanwhile, as you ponder the fluid level in your radiator and whether or not you remembered to ask for guaranteed late arrival at your motel, you'll notice that there are an inordinate number of ancient Dodge Aspen station wagons and old pickup trucks lining the soft shoulder. Parked on folding chairs under faded beach umbrellas, a variety of 3Ms (Mainers of Modest Means) peddle their wares. What wares? Well, bunches of sea grass (a lovely lavender heatherish plant) are popular, and there's always a good selection of fresh

If you find yourself stuck in the slow lane . . .

*Maine blueberries (wild ones, not the dreaded hothouse variety you probably get back home), strawberries, corn, and fiddleheads (tiny fern sprouts that are a delicacy around here). You can pick up a few pounds of fresh-caught seafood—lobster, clams, mussels, crabs, haddock, etc.—direct from the fisherman, at reasonable prices. Sometimes there are handcrafted items like whirligigs and homemade lawn art. The variety is endless. In fact, if there's such a thing as an oil on velvet painting of a lighthouse being produced in Maine, you're likely to see it here first.*

*. . . why not stop . . .*

 *Oh yeah, a big part of the fun is reading the homemade plywood signs propped up on the soft shoulder. One of my favorites, a particularly enthusiastic, "rustic" hand-lettered job on an oddly shaped rectangle of warped plywood, promises* DREM CATCHERS! $3 EACH! 500 FEET AHEAD!! *Drem catchers? It took a second to translate that. I realized as I drove by that the sign was referring to dream catchers, handmade Native American folk art. That seemed particularly fitting for this bit of highway, where the unspoken message seems to be "You too can have a tourist business in Maine." Apparently all it takes is an old station wagon, a hand-painted plywood sign, and a "drem."*

*. . . and pick up a bargain or two!*

## DOT'S GOOD DEALS
### Woolwich

It's just possible that the best "deal" you'll run across at Dot's Good Deals on Route 1 in Woolwich is a chance to shoot the breeze with Dot herself. Dot is Dot Schmidt, who has been buying, selling, and swapping just about anything you could imagine (and a few things you probably couldn't) and dickering with anyone who wanders in her door for more than twenty years now. Dot is a real "piece of work," as we say in these parts. She caught the "trash and treasure" bug early on while frequenting the state's numerous flea markets. Unlike the flea markets, however, Dot's Good Deals is open year-round. If she's not in when you stop by the shop, she's probably in the trailer next door. Go ahead and knock; it'll be worth your time whether you end up buying anything or not.

Of course, there's always plenty of stuff to paw through whenever you stop by. According to Dot, there's somewhat of a seasonal aspect to her sales. "Summertime it's your doors and windows, tubs, toilets, sinks . . . all of them go the best. . . . Bureaus, table sets. The smaller things [this could be anything from a scratched up Liberace LP and a turntable to play it on to a velvet painting of waifs with eyes the size of dinner plates] are 'iffy.' " According to Dot, "They go 'whenever.' "

What about the winter? "In the wintertime it's slower," says Dot stoically. But the wheeling and dealing never end. If you're looking for a no-dicker price, you'd be better off shopping at your local megastore. Dot's interested in more than the bottom line here, and I think her feelings would be a little bruised if her customers didn't want to haggle over the price. "That's part of the fun," she says. "If you see something you want and you can't afford the price that's on it, come up and talk to me about it."

*Come right in! Has she got a deal for you!*

For instance, she might sell a used door or commode (for some reason she always seems to have massive piles of used doors and commodes lyin' around) for less than half the asking price "to help the person that's needin' 'em. Everybody ain't rich out there," says Dot philosophically. "I've never been a rich person. But I look out for others and myself, too."

Clearly Dot isn't getting rich at Dot's Good Deals. Just as clearly she's having a pretty good time making ends meet. In fact, Dot Schmidt has darn near perfected the Yankee shopkeeper's art of mixing business and pleasure. "Most summers," she says, "I'll run my record player. I like country and western, and I've had folks come in before and say, 'C'm'ere, Dot.' So I go over, and the next thing you know they wanna dance with me. I got one older couple that comes in every year. They love Patsy Cline. They dance all the way down one aisle and up the other aisle. Then they might look around and buy something."

Besides run-of-the-mill knickknacks and used furniture, Dot's moved some pretty bizarre items over the years, including this strange artifact. "It was made of stone, and right to this day I would love to know what it really, *really* was," Dot says. "I know what they had in it. They had candles in it. But I *know* it wasn't for that. It was more 'cave man' style." The item, about 2 inches by 3 inches and a foot high, baffled even a savvy flea market veteran like Dot. "It was different," she says, adding, "It was hand done. It was the most amazing thing in the world." No dummy at dickering, Dot knew that, whether she could identify the item or not, she clearly had stumbled across something pretty special, and she held out until she got herself a "good deal." "I think I paid a hundred and a quarter for it. A guy come in from New York" (Believe me, entrepreneurs along Maine's coastal Route 1 pray annually and fervently for a good crop of these folks) "and said, 'Dot, I'll give you $1,250 for it.' "

The stone "candelabra" may or may not have been a relic from Neanderthal times. But some of Dot's "finds" have definitely had an Egyptian flavor. "Once I had a pyramid come in," she offers. "Stood prob'ly 4, 5 feet tall, covered with hundreds of buttons . . . *all different buttons*. One lady came in

and bought that and paid $250 for it." But that didn't impress
Dot as much as the fact that "all she wanted was one button!"
Dot shakes her head in amazement. You just never know. So the
next time you're passing through Woolwich, I'd recommend you
stop in at Dot's Good Deals. Whether you get a good deal or not,
you're bound to have a good deal of fun.

## EARTHA
### *Yarmouth*

**M**aine has the big stuff, all right: The Paul Bunyan statue,
the Big Indians, the objects that appear larger-than-life-
size. But what about a roadside attraction that is only
one one-millionth of its size—and yet represents something that
is bigger than anything on earth? Of course, it would have to be
a scale model of the earth itself, affectionately known as
EARTHA. It can be found spinning on its axis at the DeLorme
Map Store on the Freeport-Yarmouth line, just about a mile
south of the Big Freeport Indian.

Built in 1998, EARTHA is a giant globe, 43 feet in diameter.
According to Andy Sturtevant, public relations manager at
DeLorme, this is one one-millionth of the earth's actual diameter.
How was the earth's diameter originally measured? By overpaid
government workers with tape measures? The surface of this
globe was designed on the basis of satellite photography and
ocean studies, as well as by using information from DeLorme's
own maps. At any rate, EARTHA is so big that you can spot the
State of Maine, but it does not show political boundaries (so you
can't see the New Hampshire toll booth). You might not even be
able to tell how to get to East Vassalboro.

At night EARTHA lights up and appears, to people on the
road, to be floating. Actually, it's spinning on its own axis,

*Right around midnight this place starts to look like a scene
from a Steven Spielberg flick.*

which has different time settings for rotations. Andy says the actual rotation time of one day would be too slow to be interesting, so EARTHA rotates once every seventeen minutes. Talk about time flying by! Hey, it's 2:17 P.M. and another day has gone by.

EARTHA is part of the EARTHA Educational Alliance, a project that teaches kids about maps. In an earlier time, all we knew about maps was what we learned from the fold-out maps sold at gas stations. In these new, enlightened times, maps are more accurate and complex. One thing that has remained the same, however, is that they are still impossible to fold up properly on the first try—unless you have attended the EARTHA Educational Alliance. Andy says kids really love to visit EARTHA. Some of them aren't sure what it is and say, "Hey mom, look at the big ball."

There haven't been any reports of inaccuracy of topography (say, like making Greenland bigger than South America or putting Florida next to the Georgia that really belongs next to Russia). There also haven't been any protests from the Flat Earth Society, which plans to put its own version of the world on a less-traveled road. Andy says that several visitors have speculated that EARTHA was constructed from a do-it-yourself "kitt." (Eartha Kitt, get it?) Great minds think alike.

As for the future, don't expect a Sun, a Moon, or a Mars-tha. EARTHA was the vision of David DeLorme, and, according to Andy, David has mixed feelings about the project. "He'll take the best offer for it," Andy says. Which raises the question, who would move it? Atlas Van Lines?

EARTHA is open to visitors at no charge whenever the DeLorme Map Store is open. You can visit EARTHA seven days a week from 8:30 A.M. to 8:00 P.M. in summer and during somewhat abbreviated hours in the winter. You don't have to leave Maine to see the entire world!

# THE YORKS AND THE BERWICKS

O ne of the first things people used to see when
entering the state of Maine from New Hampshire on
Route 95 was a big green sign, resembling the other
green signs on the turnpike, which directed people to the
next exit in order to see "The Yorks and The Berwicks."

Over the years, many questions have been raised
about this sign. Basically, the questions boil down to
one: Who the heck are the Yorks and the Berwicks? Here
are some, chosen at random, from index cards left at
the tollbooth.

• Maine is, after all, the home of giants—the Walking
  Serviceman, Sardineman, the Big Indians, and others.
  Was there an entire race of people so big that they
  earned their own sign on the turnpike?

• Was Maine so small that every family had its own
  sign?

• Do you have to pay extra to have your family name on
  the sign?

• Weren't these the two feuding families in one of those
  Shakespearean plays? Did they ever intermarry?
  Would a youthful York be shot if he was seen making
  eyes at a bashful Berwick?

• There has been some speculation that if one, in fact,
  took the exit, one might soon end up in the town of
  York. Was this a town named after the people who are
  on this sign?

• If one took the exit, drove through about three other
  towns, and didn't end up back in New Hampshire, one
  might be in South Berwick, which is actually southeast
  of Berwick and nowhere near North Berwick. In which
  of these towns, if any, do "the Berwicks" live?

Times have changed, though, and the Yorks and the Berwicks are no longer on the same sign. In fact, the Berwicks are pretty much ignored these days. The towns are exactly where they were before, so it must be that the families either moved or felt the need for some anonymity. Perhaps they concluded, "Everyone sees our sign and thinks they can just drop in."

*We originally thought of calling these towns "The Montagues and The Capulets" but we didn't have enough room on the sign.*

# INDEX

# ABOUT THE AUTHORS

**T**im **Sample** is known throughout Maine and other parts of New England for his quintessential Down East humor. He got his start in the 1970s doing a stand-up comedy act with Marshall Dodge, the co-creator of the popular "Bert and I" characters, and he later went on to record several albums with the Bert and I Company. Since then he has worked on a variety of other projects, including the book *Saturday Night at Moody's Diner* and several videos and

CDs. His "Postcards from Maine" essays have appeared on *CBS Sunday Morning* regularly since 1996.

**Steve Bither** is an attorney in Portland. He is also a founding member of the Wicked Good Band, a musical comedy group that performs at festivals and events around the state. The band has produced four albums and a video. Steve, with band members Bill Schulz, Jere DeWaters, and the late Larry Spiegel, wrote the 1985 best-seller *The Wicked Good Book*.